In a country at war there are citizens, enemy aliens, and sympathetic aliens. With regard to the Catholic Church, Joyce described himself as "an acute sympathetic alien." To say that he was merely anti-Catholic, therefore, is to oversimplify.

"Your mind is supersaturated with the religion in which you say you disbelieve," says Cranly to Stephen Dedalus in *Portrait of the Artist*. Joyce, too, was brought up in the tradition of the Catholic Church, and although he left the Church and renounced all religion, echoes of his early training sound through almost all his work. J. Mitchell Morse explores this conflict as a central theme in the works of James Joyce.

Mr. Morse shows how Joyce employed the ideas of great religious thinkers, Saint Augustine in particular, for his dramatistic theory of art, for his theory of the god-like artist, and perhaps even for his conviction of the irrelevance of moral standards to artistic judgment. In separate chapters the author details the contributions of John Scotus Erigena, William of Ockham, St. Thomas Aquinas, and St. Ignatius Loyola to Joyce's idea of art, his view of the relations of the sexes, and his social attitudes.

THE SYMPATHETIC ALIEN
James Joyce and Catholicism

JAMES JOYCE, *by Ivan Opffer, from life, 1924*
Collection of Dr. H. K. Croessmann

SYMPATHETIC ALIEN

James Joyce and Catholicism

BY J. MITCHELL MORSE

NEW YORK UNIVERSITY PRESS
Washington Square   1959

© 1959 BY NEW YORK UNIVERSITY PRESS
LIBRARY OF CONGRESS CATALOG CARD NUMBER: 59-6249
MANUFACTURED IN THE UNITED STATES OF AMERICA

TO FRANCES

"And therefore when any of these pantomimic gentlemen, who are so clever that they can imitate anything, comes to us, and makes a proposal to exhibit himself and his poetry, we will fall down and worship him as a sweet and holy and wonderful being; but we must also inform him that in our State such as he are not permitted to exist; the law will not allow them. And so when we have anointed him with myrrh, and set a garland of wool upon his head, we shall send him away to another city. For we mean to employ for our souls' health the rougher and severer poet or story-teller, who will imitate the style of the virtuous only, and will follow those models which we prescribed at first when we began the education of our soldiers."—PLATO, *Republic, 398A.*

"As Stephen looked at the big square block of masonry looming before them through the faint daylight, he re-entered again in thought the seminarist life which he had led for so many years, to the understanding of the narrow activities of which he could now in a moment bring the spirit of an acute sympathetic alien. He recognised at once the martial mind of the Irish Church in the style of this ecclesiastical barracks."—*Stephen Hero, pp. 72–73.*

"The ring man in the rong shop but the rite words by the rote order!"—*Finnegans Wake, p. 167.*

Contents

Preface   ix

  I The Heretical Tradition   3

  II Handling Sin: Augustine, *Ayenbite,* and *Ulysses*   17

  III The Erigenal Sin: Irish John   38

  IV Artthoudux and Heterotropic: Cain and Abel   45

  V The Transfused Brothers: Jacob and Esau   56

  VI Jesuit Bark and Bitter Bite: Ignatius Loyola   68

  VII Art and Fortitude: Applied Aquinas   90

VIII The Godlike Artist: Augustine Again   127

Notes   141

Index   165

The numbers in parentheses following quotations from Joyce's works refer to pages in the Modern Library editions of *Dubliners,* *A Portrait of the Artist as a Young Man,* and *Ulysses;* the second New Directions edition of *Stephen Hero;* and the Viking Press edition of *Finnegans Wake.*

Preface

IF WE FIND A GENIUS AT ALL SYMPATHETIC, WE TEND TO RE-CREATE him in our own image. One result is that geniuses who speak for a variety of temperaments tend like Valéry's Faust to lose their clarity of outline, if not their identity. "My life as I remember it," says Faust, "is blended with all those lives, no less imaginary but no less authentic, which have been attributed to me." If Joyce is each of us, what is he? It is difficult to see him if we say with complacent facility that he is all men, but it is impossible to see him if we insist that he is only one. As with all writers of the first rank, there is a temptation to think of Joyce as some sort of Neo-Platonic God. He tended to think of himself as a god or a devil or both; he was treated as such in his lifetime, and perhaps his appeal is partly due to the fact that his readers think of themselves in such terms. Readers of books are inclined to build towers to Heaven or consort with demons.

For these and for more objective reasons, one of the chief topics of discussion among students of Joyce's work is the question of his attitude toward religion in general and the Catholic Church in particular. The purpose of this book is to introduce into the discussion certain ideas developed by the church fathers and the scholastic philosophers and to indicate the use Joyce made of them. "The god whose oracle is at Delphi," said Heraclitus, "neither reveals nor conceals, but indicates." That was a humane and liberal god; this book was written with some reverence for him. It will involve the reader in a certain amount of hairsplitting, but then splitting hairs is the highest end of man. Of course, one needs a sharp instrument.

Nowadays no man splits a hair or writes a book alone. Whether this is good or bad is not to the point here, but I do wish to thank those who have helped me. To Professors Marvin Magalaner of

ix

City College, New York, and Leon Edel of New York University I shall always be grateful for their warm encouragement, sound advice, and more than generous advocacy. I owe the frontispiece to Dr. H. K. Croessmann of Du Quoin, Illinois, an enthusiastic Joycean, who allowed me to choose this picture from his large private collection. Mr. T. E. Hanley of Bradford, Pennsylvania, has allowed me to make use of his choice collection of Joyce material; the pleasure of the experience was much increased by his and Mrs. Hanley's warm hospitality. Professor Thomas E. Connolly of the University of Buffalo, Mr. Gene Magner, former curator of the poetry collection at the Lockwood Memorial Library there, and Miss Anna Russell, his successor, have courteously supplied me with photostats and microfilms of items in Joyce's personal library; Professor Connolly also introduced me to Dr. Croessmann, and has gone out of his way to be helpful in tracking down other material.

I have profited by the sensitive reading and trenchant criticism of two dear friends, scholars in other fields, whose intellectual interests are not limited to their specialties and whose lively intelligence gives their suggestions uncommon value: Neal Riemer, associate professor of political science, and Howard Cutler, assistant vice president, both of the Pennsylvania State University. Professors Carlos Baker of Princeton, Frederick J. Hoffman of the University of Wisconsin, Douglas Knight of Lawrence College, Harry Levin of Harvard, J. Hillis Miller of Johns Hopkins, and Roy Harvey Pearce of Ohio State University, have made helpful criticisms of individual chapters. The Rev. Walter J. Ong, S.J., and the Rev. William T. Noon, S.J., pointed out some stupid errors in Chapter VI; Kevin Sullivan read the chapter in manuscript and wrote me a number of suggestions. Mrs. Adaline Glasheen has generously shared with me her rich knowledge of Joyce, has radically altered my approach to the *Portrait,* and by her astringent scorn of literary criticism—"even good criticism" —has somewhat chastened my own practice of it. I am also grateful to Mrs. Jean Thorsten of Penn State, who did an expert job of retyping the notes; and to my colleague Harry Meserole and my son Jonathan, who lent me their sharp eyes for proofreading.

But the greatest debt of all is to my wife, whose lifeblood is in the book. She is a heroic woman. This is not said humorously; it will not seem a tasteless extravagance, or even an exaggeration, to those who know the circumstances.

Of course none of these people is responsible for my point of view, or for any errors in the pages that follow.

Chapters II and VI originally appeared as articles in *PMLA;* Chapters IV and VIII, in *ELH, A Journal of English Literary History;* Chapter V, in *Modern Philology* (copyright by The University of Chicago Press), and a condensed version of Chapter VII, in *The James Joyce Review* (copyright by Edmund Epstein). I thank the editors of these journals for permission to republish.

For the use of other copyright material, thanks are due the following publishers: to The Viking Press for quotations from *Dubliners* (1914), *A Portrait of the Artist as a Young Man* (1916), and *Finnegans Wake* (1939); to Random House for quotations from *Ulysses* (1934) and Saint Augustine's *The City of God* (1950); to New Directions for quotations from *Stephen Hero* (1955); to the McGraw-Hill Book Company for quotations from Edward A. Fitzpatrick's *St. Ignatius and the Ratio Studiorum* (1933); and to Librairie Gallimard, Paris, for quotations from Paul Valéry's *Mon Faust* (1946) and Paul Claudel's *Positions et Propositions* (1934).

J. M. M.

THE SYMPATHETIC ALIEN
James Joyce and Catholicism

CHAPTER I

The Heretical Tradition

"Unsheathe your dagger definitions. Horseness is the whatness of allhorse."—*Ulysses,* p. 184.

JAMES JOYCE BELONGS TO THE BRAVE THOUGH RATHER TENUOUS tradition of Catholic thinkers who have stood for the individual as against the authorities. With the single exception of Duns Scotus they have fared badly; for in the church, as in any other large institution, it doesn't pay to differ with the administration. However, not every man is an organization man; here and there, now and then, a man has such confidence in his own thought that he is quite willing to clash head-on with the whole organization, and in such cases it often turns out that he was right and the organization was wrong. Right or wrong, there were a number of individualistic churchmen before the Reformation, and the sequence of their ideas was such that without abusing the word we may say they constituted a movement toward individualism within the church. It was not in the nature of Catholicism for such a movement to succeed; its failure, signalized by the condemnation of John Wyclif as a heretic thirty-one years after his death, forced all thinkers who questioned any part of the official belief thenceforth to leave the church. Joyce was an heir of that failure. Catholicism had no room for him.

Of course Protestantism had none either. In the *Portrait,* the autobiographical Stephen Dedalus feels his mind pulled downward at the sight of Trinity College, a Protestant institution, and struggles "to free his feet from the fetters of the reformed con-

Notes to Chapter I begin on page 141.

science" (209). Later, when his friend Cranly asks if he intends to become a Protestant, he replies, "I said that I had lost the faith . . . but not that I had lost selfrespect. What kind of liberation would that be to forsake an absurdity which is logical and coherent and to embrace one which is illogical and incoherent?" (287).

But at least since Tertullian, devout minds have not been prevented from holding a belief merely because it was absurd. No great faith is needed to believe what is reasonable; the more obvious the absurdity, therefore, the more ecstatic the thrill of faith. "I believe," said Tertullian, *"because* it is absurd." Stephen does not deny Cranly's statement, "Your mind is supersaturated with the religion in which you say you disbelieve" (283). He is in fact "not at all sure" that he disbelieves (286); he thinks he may still be able to unite his will with the will of God "instant by instant" (283–284), and he feels that the Eucharist may very well be the body and blood of Christ (286–287). He has an uncommonly sensitive religious consciousness, which has caused him at least once to pray to God alone in a wood (273), and he is not repelled by such a formalization of faith as the telling of beads (171). What repels him is not God, not any possible absurdity of dogma, but the institutional coercion of the individual mind. To be bullied into expressing belief in any proposition, even though the proposition itself may be reasonable enough, is what he will not endure. As an adolescent he submits to a beating by his intellectually docile schoolmates rather than say that the pious Tennyson was a better poet than the atheist Byron (89–91); somewhat later he is repelled by a priest's assertion that Victor Hugo's writing deteriorated after he left the church and that in any case Louis Veuillot was considered by many critics to have had a purer style. It is the disingenuousness of such arguments, the denial of individual merit, the coercive direction of individual judgment, the intellectual politics, that repel and alienate him. He refuses the sacrament of the Eucharist not because he believes it is unreal but because, as he says, "I fear . . . the chemical reaction that would be set up in my soul by a false homage to a symbol behind which are massed twenty centuries of authority and veneration" (287). He renounces Catholicism not because he is irreligious but because he is anti-authoritarian. In this, Stephen is an autobiographical figure; in this, Joyce was the heir of a great movement in Catholic thought—a movement which, though it inevitably failed, prepared the way intellectually for Protestantism and democracy. An understanding of its development will help us to understand the palingenetic evolution of Joyce's own attitude toward institutional religion.

Precisely when the movement began, it would be difficult to say. As early as 851, John Scotus Erigena, in *De Divisione Naturae,* had maintained (1) that in cases of conflict between reason and authority the individual should trust reason, since valid authority was supported by reason, and (2) that since Scripture was the ultimate authority, no human authority should forbid the individual to investigate its meaning by the light of reason.[1] But Erigena lived two hundred years too soon; he was forced to burn the book with his own hands; he had little influence and no immediate successors. The movement toward individualism, on its intellectual side, grew out of the realist-nominalist controversy, which began with Berengar of Tours about 1050.[2]

The central concern of medieval philosophy was the question of universals—whether genera and species existed independently of their individual members or were merely verbal abstractions. There is no record that the question of how many angels could dance on the point of a needle was ever considered; rather, the schoolmen asked the question, Which came first, the genus *animal,* the species *horse,* or the individual horses? Just what is *equinitas?* The question is far from trivial. Are we human by virtue of our membership in the human species, or is there no such species except as a figment of the mind? Just what is *humanitas?* Our answer to this question indicates our whole social attitude. Which has priority by nature, the individual or the group? If a genus or species has objective existence, if it is a real entity and not merely a word signifying a collection of individuals, what is its nature and how is it apprehended? Is there such a thing as love, over and above particular loves? If so, what is it? Is there such a thing as justice, over and above particular just acts? If not, how do we know whether an act is just or unjust? Are there universal principles, or are there not? Are what we call principles abstracted from experience, or do they have objective existence a priori? Are they merely convenient working arrangements, subject to change with time and place, or do they have a suprahuman validity? To what extent, if any, should human affairs be governed by nonhuman standards? Should the individual be sacrificed for the principle, or vice versa? Does the organization (the government, the church, the university) exist for the sake of the individual, or the individual for the sake of the organization? Or both? Just what is their proper relationship? The relevance of such questions to our own time is obvious. Their importance and their difficulty were fully appreciated by the scholastics, and Joyce was concerned with the variety of scholastic answers.

In the Middle Ages those who thought universals were real were called *realists;* those who thought they were merely generic or specific (species) names were called *nominalists.* The universals were called *essences* or *substances;* the details of their material embodiments or individual manifestations were called *accidents.* The patron saint of realism was the Neo-Platonist Augustine; of nominalism, Aristotle. About 1050, Berengar of Tours, applying the recently discovered logic of Aristotle to an inappropriate subject, the mystery of the Eucharist, reasoned himself into a heretical position and began a controversy whose echoes are still ringing. The accidents of a thing, he argued, cannot exist without its substance; thus, if by the act of consecration the sacramental bread and wine really ceased to be bread and wine, the accidents of bread and wine could not remain; since they do remain, their substances must remain; since the substances of bread and wine remain, their transubstantiation into the body and blood of Christ is symbolic, not real. Such a view could of course not be permitted, since it tends to make the value of the Eucharist subjective rather than objective, to make the experience of the communicant more important than the ministrations of the priest, and thus to transfer spiritual power from the church to the individual. It also implies that some sacraments are of no value—infant baptism, for example, or the administration of extreme unction to an unconscious man. This might be called proto-Protestantism. Berengar's argument is recorded and answered by Lanfranc, first Archbishop of Canterbury under the Normans, in *Liber de Corpore et Sanguine Domini Nostri* (1079):

> As the Apostle Andrew says, though on earth His flesh and blood be indeed eaten and drunk, yet until the time of the Resurrection of all He shall remain whole and alive at the Father's right hand in Heaven. If you ask how that can be, I answer briefly and to the point: A mystery of the Faith can be advantageously believed; it cannot be usefully investigated.[3]

Berengar was twice forced to recant, but continued to teach his doctrine; and the question, once raised, would not down. Between 1092 and 1094 Saint Anselm, Lanfranc's successor at Canterbury, wrote *De Fidei Trinitatis et de Incarnatione Verbi* in reply to a work (now lost) by Roscellinus of Compiègne (1050–1125), professing the heresy of tritheism. Just as individuals are the sole reality and "mankind" a convention of speech, Roscellinus is supposed to have said, so each person of the Trinity is unique and independent: the Trinity is not one but three—a collection, not a self-existent entity. Anselm quotes him as having said, by way of proof,

> If in God the three persons are one substance, and not three unique and separate substances—as it were three angels or three spirits—so that in will and power they are completely the same, then the Father and the Holy Ghost were incarnated with the Son.[4]

To this, Anselm replies that a man who cannot grasp the concept of humanity can hardly be expected to penetrate the mystery of the Trinity and should not presume to discuss it.[5] The articles of faith are to be believed; if we can understand them rationally we should thank God; if we can't, we should not boast of our strength, brandishing our horns, but bow our heads in reverence.[6]

It will be observed that the arguments of Lanfranc and Anselm tend to be anti-rationalistic. In Anselm's subsequent exposition

of the Trinity—essentially the same as that in the *Monologium*—
he answers logic with logic; but instead of letting logic lead him
where it will, he makes it lead him where it should. Erdmann
has observed that Anselm was "a dialectician even in his
prayers"; [7] but he was also something of a mystic even in his
dialectics. His most personal utterances are the meditations; their
general purport is indicated by the fact that in the fourteenth,
fifteenth and sixteenth centuries some of them were attributed
to Richard Rolle.[8] In fact, it was the mystics, not the scholastic
realists, who most effectively answered the scholastic nominalists;
and they too, in their disavowal of logic and their insistence on
the overriding authority of personal experience, helped to swell
the tide of individualism.[9]

In the schools, nominalism gradually won out—though of
course it is not easy to classify the major thinkers simply as
nominalists or realists. What happened was less a victory of
nominalists as such over realists as such than an increasing tendency toward nominalism in the thinking of schoolmen generally.

In 1159 John of Salisbury, in the otherwise realistic and authoritarian *Policraticus,* asserted that it was a waste of time to
consider the problem of universals, since no final solution was
possible [10]—a view which owes much to the conceptualism of his
master Abelard—and that there were many matters on which intelligent men might admit doubt and suspend judgment, including providence, the incompatibility of fate and free will, the
virtues and vices, the nature of sin, of angels, and even of God.[11]
In the Aristotelian and half-nominalistic *Metalogicus,* a defense
of logic alike against its enemies and its frivolous friends, he
held that form without content is of no value; that we cannot
be merely logical, but must be logical about something; that
though the general is the meaning of the particular, the particular is the life of the general; that the eternal and unchanging
truth must be sought in its shifting and changing appearances;
and that the success of our researches, though never complete, is
proportioned to the eagerness, fidelity, modesty of assertion, and
freedom from preconceptions with which we pursue them.[12]

This suggested attention to particulars—one of the founda-
tions of the scientific attitude—was put into practice a century

later by Roger Bacon, whose generally nominalistic attitude is too well known to need recounting here.[13] Bacon's work in any case had little influence on his contemporaries;[14] a much greater impetus was given to nominalism by his younger contemporary Duns Scotus (1266–1308), who is generally accounted a moderate realist. The two chief points of Scotus' doctrine were (1) the primacy of the will over the intellect and (2) the uniqueness of the individual.

The human will, said Scotus, is completely free; it interacts with the intellect and may be influenced by it, but is not compelled by it;[15] nor is it compelled by God's own will. Since God is not compelled by any law superior to Himself, whatever He in His infinite wisdom and infinite goodness wills is good. For man, then, goodness consists in conformity to God's will and evil in departure from it. But if it were man's nature to conform to God's will in all things he would not be free, and sin would be impossible. Moreover, man would then be not man but God. As authorities on this point Scotus quotes Saint Anselm, Saint Augustine and Saint Jerome, all of whom agree that it is impossible for God, the Uncreated, to create Himself or beings equal to Himself.[16] Thus, by the undeniable fact of sin, we know that man is free. God can, if He so wills, make a man sinless by divine grace, but not by nature.[17]

To assert that sin is the result of freedom is to favor the heresy of Erigena over the orthodox Augustinian doctrine (which Erigena called "blasphemy") that God ordains sin for His own good purposes;[18] moreover, in Scotus' treatment the emphasis is entirely on the will of the individual rather than on the human species' tendency to sin. This is the chief point on which he differs from Saint Thomas. The Angelic Teacher had asserted that the important thing about a man is his humanity, not his individuality or his generic animality. Though each soul is unique in its form, the difference between souls is actualized only when they are clothed with matter in the human compound, matter being the principle of individuation. Thus the individual differences, though real, are temporary and deserve little consideration. Man is an animal with a soul; the important thing is the soul, which differentiates the human species from the others, and the individual has one only because he is a member of the species: "Thus it is that the intention of nature is towards the species and not the individual or the genus." [19]

No, says the Subtle Teacher, matter is not the principle of individuation. The matter of which bodies are made is identical in each; the difference is a difference not of matter but of form; each human body has its own substantive, essential form, which makes it *the* body that it is. Form being of higher dignity than matter, the difference between bodies is not unimportant; and since the soul in the human compound is also unique by virtue of its form, the individual human compound is important. Human beings are not interchangeable. No individual can be reproduced as such; each one is a new entity, physically and spiritually: "The end is not the final cause of the efficient cause, but of the effect. . . . The Composite is truly one. Therefore it has some one entity which is neither the entity of the matter nor that of the form." [20] Thus the ultimate intention of nature is not the species but the individual.

But then what becomes of the species humanity? Is the human race, as distinct from individuals, nothing but a word? Scotus meets this difficulty by asserting that the difference between one individual and another is not of nature but only of form. All souls are of the same kind, sharing a *natura communis*,[21] but each has its own individual form. Its very existence as a separate soul consists in this uniqueness, which is intrinsic and substantive, not accidental. The soul has not only *quidditas* ("whatness," spirituality) but also *haecceitas* ("thisness," selfhood, individuality).[22] It is not only *a* soul but also *this* soul, in its very essence. The body likewise has not only corporeality but also an essential individuality. A man is not only *a* human being but also *this* human being, and his *thisness* is an essential part of his nature as a man. Though Socrates and Plato are alike in that they share the *animalitas* of their genus and the *humanitas* of their species, they are different in that Socrates has his *Socrateitas* and Plato his *Platonitas,* and this difference is important. Every man is of his own genus, *sui generis,* the only one of his kind.

The implications of Scotus' conclusions are democratic and Protestant. In the thirteenth century, when society and all its institutions were organized on the Salisburian principle that the individual human being was of no importance as such, that his only significance was as a "member" of some "body"—the state, the church, the guild, the order—or some occupational estate— peasant, soldier, priest—Scotus asserted his title to be valued as an individual. It is true that a hand or a foot has no value except as a part of the organism, but Scotus rejected the metaphor on the grounds of man's free will.

His influence was enormous in his own day, and continued strong to the middle of the sixteenth century.[23] His followers even adopted his name, whose subsequent fate is a poignant irony. The Renaissance humanists bedunced him because, to their shame, they neither knew nor cared what he was talking about. But until their time his works were standard texts at Oxford,[24] and he had a pervasive influence on the thought of John Wyclif.[25] Still more influential in the schools, however, was William of Ockham (1300–1349), who carried nominalism to its logical conclusion, gave realism the knockout blow that made it ineffective until the end of the nineteenth century, directly inspired Martin Luther, and had a strong though indirect influence on Wyclif. In *Ulysses,* Joyce refers to him with evident delight (41); he could hardly feel otherwise toward him, for Ockham was one of the principal founders of individualism in social life, of positivism in ethics, of empiricism in science, and of skepticism in metaphysics.[26] He was not, however a modern man in his thinking, but a medieval Christian much like Abelard. His nominalism proceeded from a religious motive: to show the impotence of reason to reveal religious truth, and thereby to establish the independence of faith from reason.[27] Coming as late in the game as he did, it was perhaps inevitable that he should be accused of making faith seem unreasonable; and in view of his political opposition to the victorous Avignon papacy he has until recently been regarded as an enemy of religion. This misconception was due partly to the fact that we are enemies or friends of religion according as our side wins or loses, and partly to the fact that most of his works were available only in manuscript. At least half of them remain unprinted to this day.

Faith, for Ockham, was an individual matter; as long as there was one believer there would be a church, for the life of the church lay not in its institutional organization but in the hearts of its members. In the *Portrait* Cranly gives a faint, distorted echo of this view: "The church is not the stone building nor even the clergy and their dogmas. It is the whole mass of those born into it" (289–290). Ockham would have said "each of those born into it." For him the institution was merely a collection of individuals, who alone were real.[28] No institution was a self-existent entity, since the human species itself was merely a collection of individuals. This he proceeded to prove, as follows. Every single thing that exists is numerically one. If humanity exists—not as a verbal abstraction but as a real entity—it must be added to the total number of human beings in the world, as something different from them. That is an absurdity, unless we assume that the entity is distributed among all the individuals in the world. But if it is so distributed, then it is exactly the same in all individuals—and who would say that humanity is the same in Judas and in Christ? [29] (A modern man can see much poignancy in the notion, but in the Middle Ages Ockham's objection was fatal.) The only other possibility is that the entity varies from individual to individual, in which case there are as many humanities as there are people—another absurdity. No, said the Invincible Teacher, "humanity" is merely an abstraction; there is no real *natura communis,* no human nature; the species is no more than the sum of its parts:

> The universal is not some real thing having a psychological being inside the soul [like love or fear] or outside of the soul [like a table or chair]. It has only a logical being in the soul and is a sort of fiction [like the symbol x]. . . . It is impossible that an entity of reason would be objectively identical with a real entity. . . . An idea is not an existential thing.[30]

Ockham drew practical conclusions from this doctrine, which he set forth in political pamphlets against Pope John XXII on behalf of Michael da Cesena and other Franciscans who wanted their order to return to the simplicity of Saint Francis. No society, said Ockham, is superior to the individuals who constitute it. In reply to the Pope's half-nominalistic assertion that the Franciscan order had no rights against him because it was not a real but merely a fictive person, Ockham stated that there was no such thing as a fictive person: "The Minors [Franciscans] are the Order, and the Order is the Minors"; [31] the Pope, in trying to coerce the order into owning property by stripping it of its right to administer property in the name of the Holy See, had violated the rights of each Franciscan individually. A society exists only by virtue of agreement among individuals, and has no real existence apart from those individuals. They may change or modify the agreement from time to time, by assassination if no other method is permitted, and they need not submit to any human authority without redress. All human beings are subject to error, since "love and hate, anger, envy and the other passions of the soul corrupt the judgment and turn it aside from the truth." Thus, anyone who sins is liable to error, and, since in this life no man is free from sin, any man can fall into heresy. The fact that a man holds ecclesiastical office does not exempt him from this danger, however high the office. Ockham did in fact accuse the Pope of heresy. Moreover, he said, if men are fallible individually, they are fallible when assembled in council. A church council thus has no monopoly on wisdom or even on faith, since God grants wisdom and faith to whom He will. The implication, says the Catholic scholar Léon Baudry, is that church councils should be open to the laity.[32]

The seeds of Protestantism are clearly here. Luther referred to Ockham as "my master" and "my dear master"; [33] and Wyclif's final conception of the Eucharist shows the influence of Ockham's. Dr. Baudry denies the influence, saying, "The Wycliffist theory of the Eucharist does not reflect the position taken by William. William admits the dogma of the transubstantiation." [34] But William admitted all the dogmas. He only insisted that they could not be proved but must be taken on faith.[35] And Wyclif was not born with theological dissent on his lips. For most of his life he was a conservative in theology; his ideas underwent a long evolution, and were not always consistent.[36] Though an old-fashioned realist in his premises and an outspoken opponent of nominalism,[37] in his last years he reached conclusions that went far beyond those of Ockham in their implications of individualism; he could not have gone so far had the ground not been prepared, and the fact that the masters-regent of Oxford unanimously supported him indicates that it had been prepared. To point out that his conclusions were more radical than Ockham's is not to disprove Ockham's influence.

With regard to the Eucharist, Ockham had maintained in Chapters IX and X of *De Sacramento Altaris* that after the Host is consecrated its quantity and qualities remain unchanged, and therefore that the body of Christ is not in it either quantitatively or qualitatively. But he did not leave it at that; in Chapter XIII he asserted that though the Real Presence is contrary to nature, God's will is absolute and can cause a substance to exist without accidents, or accidents without their proper substance:

> No contradiction appears in the statement that an absolute thing may exist without all that which is neither a part of it nor an essential cause of it. But no accident is a cause or a part of the substance in which it inheres; therefore, no contradiction is involved in the statement that a substance can exist *per se* without an accident. . . . God has made many things wonderful and contrary to the common course of nature.[38]

This is consistent with Ockham's view that the articles of faith must be taken on faith. But Wyclif, rather than accept such a sharp conflict between faith and reason, denied that an accident could exist without a subject. Asserting that the doctrine of Berengar was the original faith of the church, he said Christ was present in the consecrated Host spiritually, figuratively, and "virtually," but not physically.[39] When this view was condemned by the Chancellor of Oxford, Wyclif appealed to the Crown; when the Crown, deciding that he had gone too far, advised him to submit, he set forth his views even more plainly in a great *Confession* dated May 10, 1381, whose implications are unequivocally nominalistic and individualistic. The bread, he said, remains bread in substance as well as accidents, and the body of

Christ, seven feet tall, remains in Heaven. It is the body of Christ that the faithful worship, not the bread, which is merely a symbol. (This is Stephen's word too.) Wyclif compares the bread to the wood of a holy image: to say that it is more than a symbol, that it is really Christ, is idolatry. The physical eye cannot see in the bread what is not physically there, but "the eye of faith" can see the body of Christ "spiritually" in the bread. The presence of Christ is no less real for being spiritual rather than physical: the "worshippers of signs" and "worshippers of accidents" are "priests of Baal." [40] (The language of religious controversy, unlike that of godless science, tends to be abusive.)

That Wyclif's poor preachers spread this doctrine throughout England is attested by the chronicler of Saint Albans: "Among other things, they say and assert that the Eucharist on the altar after consecration is not really the body of Christ but a figure of it." [41] From this they did not hesitate to draw the most unorthodox conclusions, going far beyond Wyclif's own position.[42] The English works attributed to Wyclif are of dubious authenticity, but there is a large body of Lollard tracts and sermons that present such startling ideas as these:

> The power that priests have standeth not in transubstansing of the Host, nor in making of accidents for to stand by themselves; . . . and these miracles that be feigned that no man may see nor know, as they are without profit, so they have no ground in God.[43]

Wyclif himself did not go so far; he never doubted the virtue of the sacrament, and repeatedly asserted his belief in its divine ordination; but the Lollards, in their insistence on the sole value of the individual experience, tended to do away with all outward observances, to recognize no authority but Scripture, and to admit no judge of Scripture but the individual communicant. Wyclif did imply that the only legitimate power of a priest was that which any man might exert as a morally superior person.

Thus the last of the schoolmen transmitted to the general public ideas that had been evolving in the universities for a long time. The schoolmen protested (1) against the despiritualization of religion and (2) against the devaluation of the individual person. These were precisely Joyce's reasons for leaving the Catholic Church. In all his works, as we shall see, the church is portrayed as an enemy of spiritual life and an obstacle to personal development. Ignatius Loyola, as a leader of the Counter-Renaissance, fought for the restoration of medieval values; Joyce, as a product of the system of education devised by Loyola, fought like the schoolmen with medieval weapons for modern values. As Stephen puts it in the *Portrait*, he was trying "to forge out an esthetic philosophy" in terms of the "monkish learning" he had acquired (209), in order to hit the conscience of his race (280) and bring it belatedly into the modern world. Though his mind habitually wore "the vesture of a doubting monk" (205), he was never cynical. It was rather against the cynicism of the comfortably orthodox that he revolted. In so doing he was in the tradition not of those hard-eyed Protestants who established new orthodoxies as restrictive as the old, but of the humane proto-Protestants of the Middle Ages. As Shaun says in *Finnegans Wake*, Shem is "middayevil down to his vegetable soul" (423)— the vegetable soul of Bunthorne and the vegetative soul of Aristotle. As usual, Shaun utters more truth than he understands, but his understanding is good as far as it goes. Joyce's thought was most often expressed in medieval terms. The following chapters will attempt to trace its development in those terms.

CHAPTER II

Handling Sin: Augustine, *Ayenbite*, and *Ulysses*

"And with-inne the hertes of folk shal be the bytinge conscience, and with-out-forth shal be the world al brenninge."—
The Persones Tale.

IN THE MORE HIGHLY DEVELOPED RELIGIONS THERE ARE FIVE ELEments, which, though they often occur together, are quite distinct and should not be confused: orthodoxy, or correct belief; piety, or emotional response to the deity or the doctrines or the ritual or any two or all three; mysticism, or the sense of God's immediate presence; asceticism, or denial of the animal appetites; and ethics, or good human relations. It is essential to keep the distinctions in mind when dealing with the work of Catholic writers, most especially that of Joyce; for Joyce's exasperated awareness of them was one of the impelling motives of his work. For Catholics, "sin" is a generic term covering unorthodoxy, impiety, indulgence of the animal appetites, and bad human relations; in the lay mind the distinctions among them are liable to become blurred, with resulting confusion in the conduct of life. One of the purposes of the medieval manuals of the virtues and vices, such as *Ayenbite of Inwyt, Piers Plowman,* and *Handlyng Synne,* was to remind laymen of the distinctions and the hierarchy among sins as well as of their generic sinfulness. *Ulysses* too is, among other things, such a manual; one of its principal themes is Handling Sin, as this is achieved by Dedalus and

Notes to Chapter II begin on page 144.

Bloom, each in his own way; *Ulysses* accordingly adapts the
material of *Ayenbite* somewhat as it does that of the *Odyssey*.

All such manuals owe something to the *Confessions* of Saint
Augustine, whose conception of evil is that of an artist. The
passage that floats into Dedalus' mind during the Moses-in-Egypt
oration—"It was revealed to me that those things are good which
yet are corrupted which neither if they were supremely good nor
unless they were good could be corrupted" (*Confessions*, VII, 12)
—is an expression of Augustine's basic doctrine that God, being
perfectly good, creates only good; that evil is a negative condition like darkness, cold or vacancy, a lack of being: "For evil has
no positive nature; but the loss of good has received the name
'evil.' [1] . . . Therefore, if things shall be deprived of all good,
they shall no longer be. So long therefore as they are, they are
good: therefore whatever is, is good." [2] From this it is a short
step in one direction to Saint Anselm's static doctrine, "If therefore things are what they are, . . . they are without doubt what
they should be," [3] and a few steps in another direction to Walt
Whitman's confident evolutionism; both attitudes are subsumed,
under the influence of Augustine's discussions of time and memory, in Joyce's ultimate *Lebensbejahung* as priest of the imagination. Good, in this context, is aesthetic rather than moral, cosmic
rather than human. The church has never used this doctrine to
excuse bad behavior, except on the part of rulers divinely appointed as agents of God's inscrutable will; [4] neither does Joyce
deny that behavior may be bad in human terms; like the church,
he denies the existence of an over-all evil principle in the universe or an over-all evil purpose in human history; but he goes
one step further and denies that there is an over-all good purpose
either. His universe is morally neutral—a condition impossible
for human beings to attain. Thus human misdeeds, though they
may be crimes, are not sins: the universe is not offended. Man,
being offended, is not at home in the universe. Joyce, in stating
this fact, deprived morality, in his own eyes, of its traditional
sanction in the nature of things; and though he was by no means
the first to state it, he did thereby cut himself off from the majority, who need the support of such a sanction. He was himself
offended by human misdeeds, but not as an artist; what the

church condemned as sins, he used as material for his work; and every artist enjoys his material. Insofar as *Ulysses* is autobiographical, it is another portrait of the artist as a young man, the author standing at ten to seventeen years' distance from his subject. To this extent Joyce achieved his ideal of the godlike artist. Only in *Finnegans Wake* did he express his mature, contemporary conviction, revealing himself (by the act of writing the book as well as by its content) as less a god than a titan—what Michel Carrouges would call an antitheist. But antitheism, unlike atheism, is a form of religion. In religion as in literary style, Joyce's development was continuous, and *Ulysses* must be read as the expression of a stage in his development—the climactic stage of liberation from remorse.

When Dedalus, the Son, having refused all comfort, parried all questions, taken no counsel but his own, and made no promises but to himself, walks forth at last a man, Bloom, the watchful Father, sinks into prenatal sleep, "the manchild in the womb" (722). Previously Dedalus has been haunted by the voice of Icarus crying "Father!" as he fell (208). Stephen achieves maturity by learning to fall, if he must fall, without crying "Father!"—"My tumble," says the Gripes, "is my own"—and in the death-through-maturity of God the Son, as Frazer tells us, God the Father is reborn. Dedalus is Dedalus at last: the individual, the free man, the adult, the creator. The virtue of the uncreated Creator and unmoved Mover is that It is not subject to influence. The artist aims at this condition of pure creativity; this is Dedalus' quest throughout the novel.

Bloom too, though he is no artist, will bloom again by freeing himself from the mean influences about him. He seeks a mode of life as Stephen seeks a mode of art—a task equally difficult, though for different reasons. Perhaps unconsciously responding to Simon's (the original Pope's or Papa's) deadly feat of marksmanship (607), he demands "a couple of eggs" for breakfast, proposing a more fruitful use of them (723); and Molly's answer, as it was sixteen years ago after giving him the seedcake from her mouth, is "Yes." For her sake as well as Bloom's and his own, Stephen must not stay with them. As his intellectual independence dates from his refusal to enter the church, so his social independence dates from his refusal to enter the family. He rejects the inefficacious sacrament of the cabmen's shelter ("something in the shape of solid food, . . . a bun, or so it seemed," and "what was temporarily supposed to be called coffee" [606]); in Bloom's home, since cocoa is a food, not a drug or a deception, he does accept cocoa, but immediately afterward destroys any possible effect of communion his acceptance may have had by singing a song which he knows will be offensive—an act which, considering where he is, violates the relationship of host and guest (674–676). An artist must not accept help if any advice goes with it. Nor must he be grateful. As far back as "The Day of the Rabblement" Joyce has warned against the temptations of the popular devil, and the hero of *Stephen Hero* rejects the Jesuits' offer of help: "Don't you think they were trying to buy me?" (228). Like Stephen, Joyce has an obsessive fear of becoming obligated, of being bought, whether by home, fatherland, church, or any other nurse, however kindly; for to be served by an institution whose purpose is to serve is to serve its purpose; especially for the artist, to be served is a stricter slavery than to serve. "Your puddin is cooked!" Shaun roars at Shem in *Finnegans Wake*. "You're served, cram ye!" (424). But Shem (Joyce) will neither serve nor let serve. The abode of bliss presided over by the whore of Babylon is not for him, whatever it may call itself.

The traditional roles of Father and Tempter are thus combined. The helpful Bloom is for the moment a tempter, since each man must save his own soul in his own way; but the Arch-Tempter is Stephen's foil, Mulligan, mass man who scorns the mass, mocking priest, wounding healer, and unbelieving conformist. He is the well-adjusted popular devil, perfectly amenable to "every flattering influence of vanity and low ambition." [5] Properly speaking, he has no pride. Though arrogant and overweening, he lacks the self-confidence of Lucifer or Aristotle's proud man, of Dedalus, or of Bloom. He is not exiled from Heaven, because he was never in it; having no integral consciousness, being an object without a subject, he cannot will to serve, consent to serve, or refuse to serve; nevertheless he serves, even while he mocks, as a force of nature serves purposes of which it is not aware. *Was Du verlachst wirst Du noch dienen* (195). His

mockery is a manifestation of that lack of vision which, spiritually, is a lack of being. But Stephen, the Son, in refusing to be
identical with the Father, does not become a fatuous mocker;
rather, he manifests the vice of pride, head and fount of all sins
and all creativity, and so becomes the Enemy, the self-willed
exile. The original sin was to assert one's individuality, to make
a choice different from that of the Father. Satan could return to
Heaven if only he were willing to fit in, and Erigena assures us
that eventually he will; [6] but then of course he will no longer
be Satan. This doctrine—as Erigena doubtless came to see from
his own experience—yields no comfort to the nonconformist. For
the godlike creative spirit the return from exile is not satisfactory; he is never less at home than when at home, in exile
from exile. But the conviction of sin, first and last link with the
community of saints, is not easily cast off; if Dedalus has affinities
with Tennyson's Ulysses, he also bears a striking resemblance to
Orestes:

> *Iphigenia:* May I not ask if thou art King of Argos?
> *Orestes:* Not King but exile. Menelaus is King.
> *Iphigenia:* What? In thy time of grief he banished thee?
> *Orestes:* Not he but Furies—the avenging Fiends!
> *Iphigenia:* Thy madness on the beach—it was the Fiends?
> *Orestes:* Yes, yes! One seeing me might think me mad.
> *Iphigenia:* And they pursue thee for thy mother's death?
> *Orestes:* To catch me and to curb me with her blood.[7]

Dedalus' problem is to avoid being caught and curbed, to
make wings of the nets that are flung at him. Mulligan accuses
him of having killed his mother (8), and there is enough truth in
the accusation to entangle him, but only temporarily—only until
he learns how to use it in a work of art, a process that converts
both sin and accusation into elements of beauty. Joyce was fasci-
nated by Saint Augustine, who thought of God as an artist:

> For God would never have created any, I do not say angel,
> but even man, whose future wickedness He foreknew, unless
> He had equally known to what uses in behalf of the good

He could turn him, thus embellishing the course of the ages,
as it were an exquisite poem set off with antitheses.[8] . . .
God, supremely good and supremely just, grudges no beauty,
whether it be produced by the soul's damnation, or retreat,
or perseverance.[9]

Certainly this is consistent with Stephen's—and Joyce's—notion
of the artist as analogous to God, "invisible, refined out of existence, indifferent" *(Portrait*, 252)—a notion that has much in
common with Flaubert's repeated statement that the author in
his work must be like God in the universe, present everywhere
and visible nowhere, above personal feeling, all-powerful but
silent, astonishing the beholders of his work by his impassivity.[10]
This Neo-Platonic God is not a member of the community of
saints, and the artist, as artist, which is to say as instrument of
God, is not a member but a detached observer of society. As long
as he is true to his own observation, whatever he does is right.
If society binds him to itself and commits him to its values
through a conviction of sin, he must, as artist, overcome that conviction. But since he cannot cut himself in two, he must overcome it as a man; and the effort to overcome it—whether by
transcending it in a safely orthodox fashion, as in the case of
Eliot, or by transcending it in some unorthodox fashion, as in
the case of Baudelaire, or by rejecting it, as in the case of Joyce
—this effort is the substance of his work. The artist does not become God, but he tries. Joyce, having found himself morally unable to subordinate intellect to faith, as Eliot did, or to seek
virtue in degradation, as Baudelaire did, could free himself of
the sense of sin as society understood it only by denying the concept of sin as society understood it, and establishing for himself,
as godlike artist, a completely different scale of values. All his
work is the record of a struggle to do this, to overcome the per-
sistent influences of his upbringing. It was a lifelong struggle. "I
am a product of Catholicism," said Stephen Hero; " . . . I cannot in a moment destroy every feeling in my nature. That takes
time." (139). In time, as we shall see in Chapter IV, Joyce over-
came the strong feeling of piety that is so evident in the *Portrait*
(273); during the years when he was writing *Ulysses*, however, his

religious attitude seems to have combined piety with unorthodoxy.

For if he was to be an instrument of God he could not be an instrument of the church. He would have to work in his own way. He asserted the godlike element in man: the free will, the personality, the individual self, which it is the business of holiness to protect from violation. Holiness is in fact nothing but the stubborn will that will not be violated. In this sense, Satan is holy, partakes of the nature of God, and in being himself glorifies God. This is unorthodox but not impious. It is the conformists who are impious; it is society that is wrong.[11] The Englishman Haines, in saying, "History is to blame" (22), disavows all responsibility, personal and national; makes himself and his nation helpless instruments of a suprapersonal force, and so destroys all personality. Mulligan destroys it by refusing to take his own ("I'm inconsequent") or anyone else's seriously (11). For the artist this is the sin of sins; Dedalus and Bloom are holy men in that they are not guilty of it. Under whatever difficulties, with whatever waverings and lapses, each cherishes his inner self, and insomuch is honest and creative, an instrument of God. This, Stephen had recognized in the *Portrait,* was "the end he had been born to serve" (191, 196).

Dedalus does have many social sins on his conscience—almost the whole catalogue of *Ayenbite of Inwyt*—and he is absolved from them (in *Ulysses*) by refusing to take communion. That is the act of renunciation that purifies and frees the artist in him. By it he achieves the detachment that is essential both to the artistic and to the religious nature. The degree of freedom he achieves is due partly to the fact that he himself, for his own reasons, contemns all vices but the pride of Lucifer. The others —gluttony, lechery, sloth, avarice, envy, wrath—are at least as inimical to the artist as to the priest, and Dedalus' attitude toward them is more severe than that of orthodoxy itself. The fact that he compares Mulligan to Photius (22, 195), a bigger and better man, indicates a strong traditional Catholicism. His freedom is that of an adept.

Bloom too has a conviction of sin, but he must achieve absolution in a different way. Renunciation is for those who have

something to renounce. Bloom's life is ruled by a pattern easier
to contrive but harder to live with than renunciation: substitution. For the normal expression of the sexual impulse, which he
can no longer manage, he substitutes abnormal expressions; for
the other aspects of married life, in which also he is a failure, he
substitutes a charitable intervention in the affairs of Mrs. Dignam and of Dedalus; for success in business he substitutes
dreams of large-scale enterprise; for artistic expression, vague
plans to write fiction for the popular press; for education, mne-
motechnic and popular science; for Judaism, a nominal Christianity; for Christianity, undogmatic good will; for political conviction, undefined liberalism. He neither renounces anything
nor has anything; he is neither detached nor engaged. Like the
child Dedalus on the football field, he pretends to be participating; unlike Dedalus, he wants to participate. For this reason,
as well as for the reason that he has made the commitments of a
family man, he can save his soul not by renouncing society and
its values but only by participating fully in some of its activities.
He can be saved only by being accepted on some of his own
terms; Dedalus can be saved only by overcoming the need for
acceptance. These are the two ways of absolution from sin; each
has its attractions; the difficulty is to choose and to stand by one's
choice.

The sins, however, are the same in either case. All sins, says
Saint Augustine, can be summed up under three heads: the lusts
of the flesh, intellectual curiosity, and pride.[12] Almost everything
Bloom does or enjoys is a sin. Almost everything Dedalus does
or enjoys is a sin. In this, however, they are not alone; all Dubliners, knowingly or unknowingly, bear the Christian's burden.
Those who sink under it into damnation, however, are not the
Blooms or Dedaluses but the thoughtless ones, the Mulligans,
Lenehans, Punch Costellos, and Father John Conmees. All take
it up at breakfast, the thoughtful and the thoughtless alike, the
comparatively free and the wholly bound: "For by eating and
drinking," says Saint Augustine,

> we repair the daily decays of our body. . . . But now the
> necessity is sweet unto me, against which sweetness I fight,

that I be not taken captive; and carry on a daily war by
fastings. . . . This hast Thou taught me, that I should set
myself to take food as physic. But while I am passing from
the discomfort of emptiness to the content of replenishing,
in the very passage the snare of concupiscence besets me. For
that passing, is pleasure, nor is there any other way to pass
thither, whither we needs must pass. . . . And oft it is un-
certain, whether it be the necessary care of the body which
is yet asking for sustenance, or whether a voluptuous de-
ceivableness of greediness is proffering its services. . . .
Placed then amid these temptations, I strive daily against
concupiscence in eating and drinking.[13]

The sin of the mouth, says *Ayenbite,* is twofold: gluttony and
evil speaking. Dedalus fights against both of these; Mulligan is
hopelessly sunk in both. "The glutton," says *Ayenbite,*

. . . maketh his god of a sackful of dung, his belly, that he
loveth more than God, and him believeth, and him serveth.
. . . The devil . . . saith to him, "Thou eatest not for lust
of thy body, but to serve God. Thou shalt keep up the strength
of thy body for God, as David saith." . . . These reasons
are so convincing that the wisest and holiest men are sometimes caught.[14]

This vice produces five sins: eating before due time because of
"the lechery of the throat"; eating and drinking "too much and
without measure"; eating too fast, "like a dog"; wasting money
on superfluous eating; and devoting a great deal of time,
thought and energy to the business of eating.

During and immediately after breakfast, Mulligan is guilty of
all these sins, together with the ten sins of evil speaking: idle
talk, boasting, flattery, seduction, lying, perjury, strife, grudging,
opposition, and blasphemy. His first words, the Introit of the
day, combine irreverence with bad grammar, a violation of the
Word: "Introibo ad altare Dei" (5). In the next succeeding sen-
tences he mocks the Jesuits, the military, the church, science,
the prophet Malachi, the Greek spirit, the rules of prosody, the

English as a race, Oxford, the arts, the sea, motherhood, and his friend (5–10). The only things he takes seriously are his shaving and Dedalus' unsocial appearance and behavior. He tries to sell Dedalus' epigram to Haines: "I told him your symbol of Irish art. He says it's very clever. Touch him for a quid, will you? A guinea, I mean" (12). At breakfast he is gratuitously blasphemous: "The grub is ready. Bless us, O Lord, and these thy gifts. Where's the sugar? O, jay, there's no milk" (13). He is genuinely angry about the lack of milk, refuses to drink the tea without it, scorns Dedalus' indifference, and when the milkwoman appears outside is overjoyed. Having recovered his good humor, he tells a dirty joke, mocks literary scholarship, and treats the milkwoman with affable condescension—a manifestation of the vice of pride in a low form. He delivers a lecture, brief but loud, on food as physic; stuffs his mouth so full he can't talk; insists on a swim, gossips about other people's lovemaking, looks forward to a good lunch, and deftly usurps the key to the tower (14–24).

This last is a manifestation of the vice of avarice, as are also his appropriating the servant's mirror, his efforts to get money from Haines through Dedalus, and his failure to pay the milkwoman twopence that he owes her, though he can and does borrow twopence from Dedalus for a pint of beer. Dedalus, shortly before taking leave of him, consigns him to Hell along with the whole brood of mockers, notably Arius, who asserted that the Son was less than the Father; Valentine, who denied that the Word was made flesh; Sabellius, the original unitarian, who denied the personality of the Son; and Photius, a layman who, having accepted the Patriarchate of Constantinople as an instrument of secular politicans, was threatened with eternal damnation by Pope Nicholas I: "Flee therefore the dominion you have unworthily usurped." [15] Dedalus is amused at the exuberance of his own seeming orthodoxy: "Hear, hear. Prolonged applause. *Zut! Nom de Dieu!*" He is pious but free (22).

Mulligan, being neither, can only follow his nature blindly. Entering a restaurant for lunch with Haines ("the panthersahib and his pointer" [45]), he informs the Englishman of the presence of Parnell's brother, and is rewarded with a *mélange,* "some scones and butter and some cakes as well." He can hardly wait: in the presence of the Englishman he helps the waitress unload the tray, and, as at breakfast, talks with his mouth full, slandering Dedalus (245). In the library he mocks Shakespeare, having nothing to contribute to the discussion (195); in the maternity hospital, with banal adolescent humor, he mocks love, marriage, medicine, birth, and the birth rate (395–396). In the library Dedalus compares him not only to Photius but to Johann Most, the anarchist, and for his irreligion calls him "pseudomalachi" (195). He lives up to this name by calling everything a mockery (5, 8, 10, 22, 565). The name can also be read "false angel" or "false messenger." He is of those whom God, according to Augustine, has predestined to be evil and to be damned, the evil being its own damnation, a lack of vision.[16]

Bloom and Dedalus are everything that Mulligan and his friends are not: individuals conscious of their individuality and struggling to maintain it. *Ulysses* is the story of a critical day in the lifelong effort of two men to *be:* to say with God, "I am." Bloom's effort is defensive: to be allowed to live a conventional life without ceasing to be Bloom. But he has already suffered two major defeats, having disavowed his Jewishness and lost his manhood. Late in the afternoon, brought to a crisis by the rage of The Citizen, he stands when others flee and reasserts his Jewishness (336). The importance of this act of defiance, however disastrous the immediate outward consequences seem to be, is indicated by the double meaning of Bloom's reflection about it later: "Got my own back there" (373). He enjoys the feeling of victory, and after some hesitation accepts its moral rightness. This is the beginning of his regeneration: "What I said about his God made him wince. Mistake to hit back. Or? No." That "No" is a victory in itself and a necessary preliminary to the "Yes" that opens Molly's monologue. Bloom's acceptance by society begins at home; more basically, it begins with his acceptance of himself. He is a superior person; only when he asserts his superiority can he begin to assume his rightful place in society.

But the ascent from the pit to the glory of the brightness is never easy. It is especially difficult for one so burdened with sin as Bloom, whose personality has been all but destroyed by his yielding to the temptation of the second-best. And since he renounces nothing, he is also distracted by the traditional temptations of the flesh and the mind. "Thou enjoinest continency from concubinage," cries Saint Augustine.

> . . . But there yet live in my memory . . . the images of such things . . . as my ill custom there fixed; which haunt me, strengthless when I am awake: but in sleep, not only so as to give pleasure, but even to obtain assent, and what is very like reality.[17]

For the ordinary man, assent and what is very like reality do not wait for sleep. His soul, says *Ayenbite,* is like a mirror, on which the devil flashes images, "be it sleeping, be it waking." [18] These images are the "ghosts" of tempting objects. Thus,

> There is lechery of heart and lechery of body. The lechery of heart hath four steps. For the ghost of fornication helpeth the fire of lechery to seize the heart: maketh first come thoughts, and likings, and imaginations of sin to the heart, and maketh think. Afterwards the heart dwelleth in such thoughts, and so delighteth, yet do they not the deed for anything. . . . The third step is the consenting of the heart and of the reason and of the will. And such consentings be always deadly sin. After the consenting cometh the desire and the great heat that they have for to sin. . . . Without clean conscience [inwyt] no chastity pleaseth God. This chastity, this cleanness, this purity requireth that men lock the heart from evil thoughts and not consent to have sinful desires.[19]

But a man given to substitutes is particularly susceptible to sinful desires. Bloom certainly—with his clandestine correspondence, his voyeurism, his French letter, his pornographic books and pictures, his lingerie fetishism, his masturbation on the beach, his masochistic fantasms at Bella Cohen's, and his guilty memory of experiments in coprophilia—lives among ghosts who distract him from the pursuit of his proper business and the re-integration of his soul.

By modern standards he is not given to "concupiscence in eating and drinking"; he is disgusted by the gluttonous eaters in the Burton restaurant (167); he lunches cleanly and briefly in Davy Byrne's on a sandwich of gorgonzola and a glass of bur-gundy (169); Davy Byrne remarks, "I often saw him in here and I never once saw him, you know, over the line," and Nosey Flynn replies, "God Almighty couldn't make him drunk" (175). Though barrels of ale pass beneath him in a barge (150) and above him in a train (78), they do not entangle him in their weaving. However, he relishes the sandwich and the wine; he en-joys the aftertaste; he dines with pleasure at the Ormond, he eats with relish the inner organs of beasts and fowls, and he is by no means indifferent to his digestive processes. By the standards of *Ayenbite,* then, he is guilty of the sin of gluttony.

"With the allurement of smells," says Saint Augustine, "I am not much concerned. . . . Perchance I am deceived." [20] *Ayenbite* too treats the sense of smell very briefly, merely stating that it is one of the five wits that let corruption into the soul: [21] "men sin oft . . . by the nose, in too much delighting in good smells." [22] If this be a sin, Bloom is a sinner indeed: he enjoys and keenly remembers the smells of melons, flowers, perfumes, soaps, lotions, drugs, cigar smoke, incense, spices, foods, dark cellars, the sea, and the various smells of women. He is even curious about the smell of his own body: "Mr Bloom inserted his nose. Hm. Into the. Hm. Opening of his waistcoat. Almonds or. No. Lemons it is. Ah no, that's the soap" (369).

"The delights of the ear," says Saint Augustine, "had more firmly entangled and subdued me; but Thou didst loosen and free me." He is still of two minds about the auditory beauty of the Psalms and other chants:

> This contentment of the flesh, to which the soul must not
> be given over to be enervated, doth oft beguile me, the

sense not so waiting upon reason, as patiently to follow her; but having been admitted merely for her sake, it strives even to run before her, and lead her. Thus in these things I unawares sin, but afterwards am aware of it.[23]

The concupiscence of the ear, however, did not greatly disturb most medieval moralists, who seem to have been less sensitive to it than Augustine. Dan Michel doesn't mention it. What he does deplore is the fact that men sin through the ear "in foolish hearing, and in gladly hearing slanderers and flatterers and scorners and liars and other fools," [24] with each of whom he deals at considerable length. In Catholic terms, the Sirens episode of *Ulysses* deals with foolish hearing even more than with the sensual delights of the ear; the sins its dramatizes are more offensive to ethics than to asceticism, even by medieval standards. Its general tone of moral irresponsibility is indicated before it begins, by the meeting of the musicians in the street: Simon Dedalus, tenor, who loafs, drinks and has himself shaved by a barber while his children go hungry; Father Cowley, pianist, who is dodging a bill collector; and Ben Dollard, base barreltone, who says of his worn-out clothes, "Bad luck to the jewman that made them. Thanks be to God he's not paid yet," and then, making use of his personal friendship with the subsheriff, arranges to have Father Cowley's Jewish creditor bilked through a technicality (241–242). In good spirits over the victory, these three enter the bar of the Ormond Hotel, where the barmaids are gossiping and giggling about men and where the boy who brings them their tea has just spoken to them with "impertinent insolence" (254). What does the ear hear in this place? Music, of course; but also the ten sins of the tongue discussed in *Ayenbite:* loose talk, boasting, flattery, lying, perjury, chiding, slander, murmuring, opposition, and blasphemy, in all their divisions and subdivisions.[25] Even the blind piano tuner, though Bloom notes his "sensitive" hand (178) and Miss Douce says she "never heard such an exquisite player" (259), is rude and obscene (246).

Throughout the episode, Bloom maintains a degree of detachment. Such of the conversation as he hears offends him; and even while yielding to the sentimental words and music of the songs he is aware of their seductiveness: "Tenors get wom" (276). This awareness is the grace that saves him; it shares the detachment of the creative spirit; no one else in the Ormond bar has it. But in the twentieth century words are addressed to the eye almost as much as to the ear, and Bloom falls into what might be called the sin of the pen: his writing to Martha Clifford is a compulsive act, the act of one who, in this respect at least, has no control over himself, whose reason yields to lust of heart. His enslavement is clearly indicated by the fact that he must lie orally to Richie Goulding (275). In denying one of his purposes, he denies part of himself; to this extent, he ceases to be, or rather manifests a lack of being.

From the modern point of view, lechery is Bloom's only major social sin. But it is expressed in many medieval ways, notably in the concupiscence of the eyes. "The eyes," says Saint Augustine,

> love fair and varied forms, and bright and soft colours. Let not these occupy my soul; let God rather occupy it, who made these things, very good indeed, yet is He my good, not they. . . . That corporeal light . . . seasoneth the life of this world for her blind lovers, with an enticing and dangerous sweetness. . . . These seductions of the eyes I resist, lest my feet wherewith I walk upon Thy way be ensnared; and I lift up mine invisible eyes to Thee, that Thou wouldst pluck my feet out of the snare.[26]

This is what *Ayenbite* calls "foul sight," [27] the beginning of lechery. Such passages throw the light of Hell on Bloom's sensuous enjoyment of shapes and colors:

> Grafton Street gay with housed awnings lured his senses. Muslin [paynim] prints silk, dames and dowagers. . . . He passed, dallying, the windows of Brown Thomas, silk mercers. Cascades [falls] of ribbons. Flimsy China silks. A tilted urn poured from its mouth a flood of bloodhued poplin: lustrous blood. The huguenots [heretics] brought that here. . . . Pincushions. . . . Gleaming silks, petticoats on slim brass rails, rays of flat silk stockings. . . . A warm human

plumpness settled down on his brain. His brain yielded. Per-
fume of embraces all him assailed. With hungered flesh ob-
scurely, he mutely craved to adore (165–166).

This empty, dark, silent passivity is at the opposite pole from the
impassivity of God; it is the ground of his submission to the
warm human plumpness of Bella Cohen, the beautiful priest, by
which his personality is all but annihilated. It is idolatry of the
crudest kind. The essence of idolatry is substitution.

At least equally obnoxious from the point of view of Catholic
orthodoxy is Bloom's intellectual curiosity. To the lust of the
flesh, says Saint Augustine, is added

> another form of temptation more manifoldly dangerous. For
> besides that concupiscence of the flesh which consisteth in
> the delight of all senses and pleasures, . . . the soul hath,
> through the same senses of the body, a certain vain and
> curious desire, veiled under the title of knowledge and learn-
> ing, not of delighting in the flesh, but of making experi-
> ments through the flesh. . . . From this disease of curiosity
> . . . men go on to search out the hidden powers of nature,
> . . . which to know profits not, and wherein men desire
> nothing but to know.[28]

From Tertullian onward, the belief that secular knowledge is
not only unprofitable but wicked has been an unbroken strand
in Christian thought.[29] The attitude of *Ayenbite* is typical:

> Learning and wisdom are things much worshipped. But if
> thou wilt be truly wise and learn high knowledge, seek the
> true goodness of God, which is grace and virtue, for that is
> the true wisdom. . . . This wisdom exceedeth the wisdom
> of the world as the sun doth the brightness of the moon.
> . . . The wisdom of the world is but folly, as Scripture saith.
> . . . [It] is the devil's wisdom.[30]

Bloom is hopelessly tangled in this snare He is curious about
everything, from the pronunciation of *voglio* (63) to the law

of falling bodies (71), from the sensations of the blind (179) to
the digestion of the gods (174). If his curiosity is not very deep,
if the only question on which he does any research is one that
gives him an excuse to look up at the mesial groove of a goddess as Moses looked up at the backside of Jehovah (198), it is
nevertheless genuine and disinterested as far as it goes. His other
sins, which derive chiefly from his habit of accepting substitutes,
he will overcome when he regains his manhood; this one, like
Augustine, he will never be able to overcome. It will permanently
mark him off from the rest of society. His triumph will lie in
forcing society to accept him as he is, a thinker and a Jew.
After rescuing Dedalus he sees his son Rudy reading from right
to left and kissing the page, an act in which faith and intellect
meet (593).

Bloom and Dedalus are higher forms of life than the other
characters. Bloom, thinker and moralist however confused, is
man; Dedalus is the creative son of man who has not where to
lay his head; both, to the extent that they realize themselves,
partake of the nature of God. The others, weltering in their
various degrees of not-being, are mere natural phenomena:
rabbits (42), foxes (60), birds (364), a seal (24). The difference
between the natural phenomenon and the godlike stranger,
though also one of degree, is so great as to be irreconcilable.
"I am" is not, after all, a very enlightening answer. One might
as well say, with the author of *Finnegans Wake,* "Such me."
It is the nature of the stranger to be misunderstood, and of the
others to misunderstand, to construe his metempsychosis as "met
him pikehoses" (152). They are doomed by their lack of vision,
their not-being, their evil, to sell him, as he is doomed by his
perceptiveness, his fullness of being, his goodness, to buy them
again. Joyce has put it clearly in *Finnegans Wake:* "He's your
change, think you methim" (232). The words "pike" and "hoses,"
being sexual symbols ("pike" is also a kind of $\iota\chi\theta\upsilon\varsigma$ or divinity),
are concrete manifestations of that essence which Dedalus, as
a young man, had already begun to seek with the help of
Aquinas and Aristotle: "the essence of beauty" (*Portrait,* 205).
Bloom too seeks it, by the empirical, inductive methods of the
common man devoted to applied science; Dedalus seeks it by

the intuitive, deductive methods of the poet, prophet and theoretician. Bloom wears mourning for the human race in the person of Paddy Dignam (82); Dedalus wears it for his mother because he is her son (20). He is "the eternal son and ever virgin" (386) (ever uncorrupted by vulgar influences), "the fire upon the altar" and "the sacrificial butter" (183) that Mulligan eats on a slit and steaming scone while communing with the enemy of his country (245). Dedalus is not only the Son but the whole Trinity, three in one and one in three: the Agenbuyer of Hamlet's buzzing conscience, who will pay back the pound he has borrowed; the entelechy or Father, whose memory is the source of continuity and identity (another Augustinian notion), and the Holy Spirit: "I, I, and I. I":

> Wait. Five months. Molecules all change. I am other I now. Other I got pound.
> Buzz. Buzz.
> But I, entelechy, form of forms, am I by memory because under everchanging forms.
> I that sinned and prayed and fasted.
> A child Conmee saved from pandies.
> I, I, and I. I (187).

The fact of his being a child subject to discipline is not inconsistent with his being God (Luke 2:51), nor is his seeming coolness toward his family (Matthew 10:37, 12:46–50; Mark 3:31–35; Luke 8:19–21, 9:61–62, 18:29–30). What keeps him from realizing his godhead is the social sense of sin that still haunts him—not only for his behavior at his mother's deathbed, but for his failure to save his sister Dilly (240), for his youthful lechery of heart and body, for his adolescent vanities and present disaffections (41). His essential sin, however, the violation of his essence, consists in not doing the work he is destined to do, not functioning, not being fully himself, not serving what as a young man he had already recognized as "the end he had been born to serve." The other sins are all subsidiary to this. Dedalus' feeling is medieval. In the evening he sinks under his burden of guilt into the glutton's sin of

drunkenness. The modern objections to drunkenness are mate-
rialistic, having to do with health, economic efficiency, highway
safety, social decorum, etc.; the medieval objections, as set
forth in *Ayenbite,* were chiefly spiritual, since the glutton serves
his belly instead of God:

> God biddeth him fast; the belly saith, "Thou shalt not,
> but eat long and late." God biddeth him arise in the
> morning; the belly saith, "Thou shalt not, I am too full.
> The church is no hare; it will wait." And when he ariseth
> he beginneth his matins: "Ah, God, what shall we eat to-
> day? Anything good?" After these matins come lauds: "Ah,
> God, we had good wine last night, and good meat too."
> Then he weepeth for his sins: "Alas, I am nigh dead to-
> night; that wine last night was too strong. My head aches:
> I need a drink." . . . Thus it cometh that such a man saith
> that he may not fast or do penance, for he saith, "My head
> is too bad." And he saith true, for he hath made it so,
> and his heart also.[31]

Joyce's hard-won temperance had essentially the same spiritual
motive as that of a medieval Christian: it was part of his refusal
to serve any end except the one he felt he had been born to
serve. That is to say, it was part of his assertion of his own being.
Likewise, Stephen's resistance to lechery is part of his effort to
say, "I am." His lapse into drunkenness and lechery at the end
of the day is a serious defeat of his artistic purpose, and his
rescue by Old Father Bloom is his emancipation from the nightmare of history, in which all time is present and all individuality
is lost. For Bloom, though not a fabulous artificer, is in his
matter-of-factness a true, or nonmedieval, Aristotelian; and his
unmitigated concreteness forces Dedalus to do what he had
earlier, in the library, urged himself to do: "hold to the now,
the here, through which all future plunges to the past" (184).
This is a clear echo of Augustine's *De Immortalitate Animae:*

> For what is done needs expectation, that it may be done,
> and memory, that it may be understood as much as pos-

sible. And expectation is of future things, and memory is of things past. But the intention to act is of the present, through which the future flows into the past.[32]

This in turn seems to owe something to the discussion of the "now" in Aristotle's *Physics*, which Augustine tells us he studied, which Joyce doubtless studied, and which bears directly on what Joyce was trying to do:

> As movement is a continuous flux, so is time; but at any given moment time is the same everywhere, for the "now" itself is identical in its essence, but the relations into which it enters differ in different connexions, and it is the "now" that marks off time as before and after. . . . Inasmuch as the point in the flux of time which it marks is changing (and so to mark it is its essential function) the "now" too keeps changing, but inasmuch as at every moment it is performing its essential function of dividing the past and future it retains its identity.[33]

Thus "the now, the here," the white light still and moving, is the entelechy of history, which retains its identity under ever-changing forms (187). To express this fact fully is to impose order on history and awake from the nightmare. To express: not merely to state, but to make manifest, to reveal concretely in some mode of life or art. This is to be godlike—uncreated and creative, the Word that was in the beginning, the conscience of the race.

The first step is to understand the now, the here: "I have much to learn," says Stephen, who before meeting Bloom is already attempting to feed his intuitions by means of an Aristotelian concern with the details of Dublin life. As the first stage of his work, he wants to establish the objective correlatives of his epiphanies: to gather facts and set them forth in a plain style. But for a young man whose mind has been trained to the figures of scholastic rhetoric a plain style is difficult to achieve. A style of studied meanness is not the same thing at all. Joyce shows his awareness of this by parodying the

style of *Dubliners* in the story of the virgins on Nelson's pillar.
Nevertheless, the method affords him a Pisgah sight of the fulfillment of his promise, and his faith in it is confirmed by the
moral insight of Bloom, which is the soul, the radiance, the
quidditas of Bloom's concern with the *haecceitas* of things.
Dedalus and Bloom have one thing in common: moral insight,
which is a matter of being able to see the facts. This ability is
as difficult to achieve as a plain style, and for the same reason.
It is a matter of honesty with oneself, which is the most difficult
of all intellectual achievements. Dedalus, being more intelligent
than Bloom, is more perceptive of the total situation and thus
more honest with himself. That is why he refuses Bloom's invitation to live with him, which proceeds from a sentimental
failure of insight. Aside from their honesty, their desire for
freedom, they are too different to live together satisfactorily.
Dedalus, in any case, cannot consent to be served. Bloom will
doubtless recognize this fact in the morning, when Molly begins
once more to serve him.

CHAPTER III

The Erigenal Sin: Irish John

"Every artist loves his own handiwork more than that handiwork if it were to come to life would love him."—Aristotle, *Nicomachean Ethics*, IX, 7.

IN BOTH *Ulysses* AND *Finnegans Wake*, JOYCE PARTIALLY ADOPTS John Scotus Erigena's heretical view of the relations of the sexes. The narcissistic and homosexual impulses of Joyce's characters are more than accidental and more than merely perverse; they are inevitable expressions of man's nature as Erigena conceives it and a motive force of history as Joyce conceives it. In the night world of *Finnegans Wake* we are addressed as "Gentes and laitymen" (152) or "laities and gentlenuns" (177). In *Ulysses*, Molly, who gives the young-life-giving seedcake to Bloom from her mouth (173, 767), has that much in common with the virgins who give seeds from their mouths to Dublin's citizens from the top of Nelson's pillar (146). The giving of seeds is of course the male function; the virgins, casting theirs on the ground, repeat the sterile sin of Onan. On the other hand, the adjective "onehandled," applied to the adulterer, suggests the "one-handled urn" of "Gas from a Burner," a chamberpot, a receptacle, a female symbol; and certainly Bloom's act of receiving the seedcake is a female act. The eating of the Reverend Mr. MacTrigger's testes by the cannibal chief (169–170), Mrs. Breen's belief that her husband's insanity is aggravated by the new moon (155), Bloom's sympathetic quasi-menstrual suffering (332, 363) and wish to be a mother (484), Shakespeare's

Notes to Chapter III begin on page 146.

being overborne in a ryefield by Anne Hathaway (194), the transmogrification of Bella Cohen into Bello (518ff.), and the apparition of Black Liz, the clucking rooster (549), also indicate that blending of the male and female principles which is the heart of the erigenating in *Finnegans Wake* (4).[1]

Much of Erigena's philosophy is orthodox Dionysian Neo-Platonism, and in view of the pervasive influence of Neo-Platonic notions in European thought [2] it would be easy to overestimate the particular influence of Erigena on Joyce; but Erigena's heresy was his own, and Joyce's use of it, though tacit, is unmistakable; for if one of Joyce's themes is the essential unity of history, another is the history-making interaction of contraries, most fundamentally the male and the female; and one of Erigena's heretical conclusions is that the human personality, divided into sexes by sin, will ultimately be reintegrated in Heaven. Joyce denies this conception, because it is a religious conception; but his characters do have an elemental urge to unity. All that is lacking is its fulfillment. Joyce is concerned with time on earth, not with eternity.

Man's first disobedience, though not willed by God, was according to Erigena a manifestation of the divine all-inclusiveness, and thus a permissible assertion both of man's nature and of God's: "Of manifest 'tis obedience and the[e]. Flute!" (343). The fluting priests of error would be barred from Plato's city [3]—a modest proposal more misunderstood than Swift's; of course, says Joyce, they are the fruitful ones, the creators; and though in being creative they usurp God's role, they do not violate God's will; for one of the means by which God has chosen to express Himself, says Erigena, is the free will of man, the godlike attribute that distinguishes him from the rest of nature, and freedom involves the possibility of error.[4] The first exercise of Adam's will was in fact to turn away from the source of being to its manifestations, from substance to shadow, from life to death. This first assertion of godlike independence was of the nature of usurpation. "My tumble," says the Gripes, "is my own." *"Your* temple, *sus in cribro!"* bellows the outraged Mookse, who is not God but the church (154–155). The vice of pride, head and fount of all sins and all creativity, the urge to express or develop oneself in human terms, and the concomitant turning of the eyes downward to created beings rather than upward to the creator, was from the orthodox point of view an error of judgment, the intellectual dullness in which, according to all good Platonists, all sin consists. Thus Adam fell, according to Erigena, before he was tempted: otherwise he would not have been available to temptation any more than Christ was when Satan tried Him. Adam's tumble was his own; in desiring knowledge he overstepped the limits of the *cribrum*. The story of his expulsion from Paradise is merely an allegorical representation of his self-expulsion from the spiritual Paradise of communion with the Godhead.[5] But from this primordial act of self-assertion, says the anti-Platonist Joyce (blending Christian orthodoxy with existentialism and the life-giving division of the egg with the Promethean faith of the liver)—from this original schism flow all man's works, including his own nature: *"Mon foie,* you wish to ave some homelette, yes, lady! Good mein leber! Your hegg he must break himself" (59). "Homelette" is both a little human being and a little home; "ave" is both a reverent greeting and, since it means "bird," an irreverent comment ("Listen to the mocking bird"). The price of creativity is terrible; those who make civilization and domesticity possible must themselves lose all peace and quiet. By turning away from the divine and eternal unity, says Erigena, Adam plunged into time, space, diversity, change, and mortality. The human body as we know it, changeable and mortal, is the result of Adam's sin. To that same sin are due all human changes, waverings, uncertainties, differences and disagreements—including even the difference between the sexes. The sleep (*dormitio*) into which Adam was thrown was an outward manifestation, for his and our instruction, of the drowsiness (*sopor*) of his soul both before and after (following impulse rather than reason) it turned away from the source of light; the creation of Eve from his side was an outward manifestation of his loss of spiritual wholeness (*integritas*):

> And thus he was split into two sexes, masculine and feminine: which splitting took its cause not from nature but from vice. . . . That drowsiness was both the cause and the

result of sin. . . . Whence we observe that Scripture intro-
duces the feminine condition after Adam has fallen asleep,
thereby intimating to us that if human nature had not by
the irrational motion of its free will abandoned the simple
and full integrity with which it was constituted in the
image of God, but had remained always in unchanging contemplation of truth, it would by no means have become
liable to splitting into two sexes as are the irrational animals, but would be multiplied in its own way, as the number
of angels is multiplied, without sex.[6]

Christ, the second Adam ("O foenix culprit!" [23]), was in His
human aspect as uncorrupted as the first had been before the
fall: "In the first Adam nature is split into masculine and feminine; in the second it is made one. In Jesus Christ is neither
masculine nor feminine. In the first, universal nature is expelled
from the felicity of Paradise; in the second, it is recalled and
restored to that felicity." [7] (Such felicity the creative spirit rejects.
"My velicity," says the Gripes, "is too fit in one stockend" [154].)
And since the resurrection of Christ prefigures the ultimate resurrection of man in "the simplicity of pristine nature," without all
the unworthy superadditions incurred by Adam's sin, it is not
to be believed that the sexual organs will be resurrected.[8] ("O
foolish cuppled!" [433].)
   This is heretical in its conclusion,[9] but perfectly orthodox in
its assumption that sex is shameful. Joyce's training having been
what it was, he could never quite disabuse himself of the same
assumption. In all his work except the conventional poetry and
the imitative *Exiles,* sex is represented as perverse and sordid
animality. Stephen Dedalus' "sane and conscienceless acceptance
of the animal needs of young men" in *Stephen Hero* (151) is replaced by terrible remorse and mad libertinism in the *Portrait,*
and by disgust in *Ulysses.* One of the recurring motifs of *Finnegans Wake* is the snickering, lisping, stammering, circumlocutory
awkwardness with which sex is discussed or alluded to:

Face at the eased! O I fay! Face at the waist! Ho, you fie!
(18). . . . he next went on . . . to drop a few stray re-

marks anent their personal appearances . . . gently reprov-
ing one that the ham of her hom could be seen below her
hem and whispering another aside as lavariant that the hook
of her hum was open a bittock at her back to have a sideeye
to that, hom (431).

This fact, and the fact that sex so often takes perverted forms in
Joyce's work, can be explained in terms of Erigena's doctrine
that Eve was in every sense a part of Adam's self, with which he
yearned to be reunited. Earwicker's secret lust for his daughter
is more than merely incestuous, for she is also his wife, as Eve
was Adam's daughter. On this view, all sexual relationships are
essentially narcissistic and there is no such thing as complete or
genuine heterosexuality. Nature as we know it is inherently
perverse, having been corrupted in the first man when he was
the whole human race. This is orthodox enough; but Joyce, like
Erigena, includes and goes beyond orthodoxy: "Now let the
centuple celves of my egourge . . . by the coincidence of their
contraries reamalgamerge in that identity of undiscernibles
where the Baxters and the Fleshmans may they cease to bidivil
uns" (49-50). Richard Baxter, chaplain to Cromwell's Parlia-
ment and foe of the Cambridge latitudinarians, divided men
ruthlessly into the saved and the damned, but Fleischman with
his yeast would leaven the whole lump and save us all, cheerily
calling, "What'll you have?" Each of the first two syllables of
"bidivil" signifies division, and the German "uns" implies unity.
    The "coincidance" of the contraries, however, is suggested
throughout *Finnegans Wake* by the interweaving of HCE and
ALP, "the hen and crusader everintermutuomergent" (55). "*Tout
est sacré pour un sacreur, femme à barbe ou homme-nourrice*"
(81). Sometimes HCE is feminine: "Houri of the coast of emer-
ald" (68). "How charmingly exquisite!" (13). Sometimes ALP,
running forward or backward, is masculine: "Anna loavely long
pair of inky Italian moostarshes" (182). "Nor needs none shaft
ne stele from Phoenicia or Little Asia to obelise on the spout"
(68). Sometimes the sexes seem to "reamalgamerge": "Call her
calamity electrifies man" (207). Sometimes their initials are
twined in such combinations as HPE, HPC, HCP, ELC, PHAC,

HALPHALC, ACL, HAEH, CA, ACHL, HCPP, APLPLLAECH, and HHHALPLAPCCCHC: "He was poached on in that eggtentical spot" (16). "How paisibly eirenical" (14). "Her crown pretenders" (252). "Hagios Colleenkiller's prophecies" (409). "Her Parisienne's cockneze" (102). "You remember Essie in our Luna's Convent?" (27). "Princesome handsome angeline chiuff" (239). "He addle liddle phifie Annie ugged the little craythur" (4). "*Headmaster Adam became Eva Harte's* toucher" (251). "CelebrAted!" (421). "Ab chaos lex" (518). "A hairclip and a clackdish for Penceless Peter" (210). "A plainplanned liffeyism assemblements Eblania's conglomerate horde" (614). "Before he fell hill he filled heaven: a stream, alplapping streamlet, coyly coiled um, cool of her curls" (57).

To Joyce, however, the individual human soul, incomplete though it might be, was all-important, and he resisted those who would make it conform to a pattern even for the sake of salvation. He had the light-bearing pride of the artist: he preferred to be damned on his own terms rather than saved on terms his intelligence could not accept; therefore he rejected not only the salvation offered by the church but even Erigena's long-range optimism. He prefers man as man, not as a child, not even as the child of God: fallen, crippled, and doomed to eternal death, but meanwhile, however briefly and on however small a scale, independent, self-determining, and creative. For the Second Coming, in *Finnegans Wake,* he portrays Christ as an oxeyed perfidious hermaphroditic Welsh pirate from Daneland, variously known as Magnus Spadebeard and Hunkalus Childared Easterheld, whose *Heldenleben* is disastrous to strong-willed individuals: "A destroyer in our port. Signed to me with his baling scoop. Laid bare his breastpaps to give suck, to suckle me. Ecce Hagios Chrisman!" (480).[10]

Shaun, as soon as he realizes who it is, shouts, "Itch dean: . . . Hastan the vista! Or in alleman: Suck at!" (*ansuchen, aufsuchen, aufzucken, nachsuchen, ansaugen, aufsaugen*). To which Shem, a free artist who will neither be bailed out nor baled up, replies, "Suck it yourself, sugarstick" (485). Usurping the accusatory role of the Four Apostles by blending with them in Shaun's guilty dream, he rejects all blandishments (487–491) and goes down fighting: "The author, in fact, was mardred" (517). And though at the end universal nature in the person of Anna Livia rushes to lose her identity, her godlike creative son —since it is his perverse nature to live in unresolved questions —proposes the question "whither the indwellingness of that which shamefieth be entwined of one or atoned of two" (488), and so preserves his free identity. Sex, which makes shame, also makes Shem. Like Bunthorne, he is an aesthetic sham in the original sense of the word, who covers and uncovers the rude nakedness of nature. He will not serve any other cause. He declines to be the Angel of the Lord, which is to say "the engine of the load" (604). Though there be "Heinz cans everywhere" (581), he will not fit into any of them; rather he will entwine his arts with laughters low "from Ond's [evil's] outset till Odd's end" (505), the day of the universal death of all odd ones: "Till tree from tree, tree among trees, tree over tree become stone to stone, stone between stones, stone under stone forever" (259). We do not know how Erigena died, but it is said that his pious students, outraged by the boldness of his thought, closed in on him and stabbed him to death with their pens.

CHAPTER **IV**

Artthoudux and Heterotropic:
Cain and Abel

"By the original sin, man chose to be alone. . . . The son of
Adam shall no longer see anything but himself, his working
space, his land, and his shop."—Paul Claudel, *Positions et
Propositions.*

In *Dubliners,* THE *Portrait,* AND *Ulysses* JOYCE REJECTS THE
church because of its materialism; in *Finnegans Wake,* finally,
he rejects its spiritual base also. In the first three books he will
have no gods before himself; in the fourth he accepts the role of
Cain, an admittedly shady Promethean. The changed feeling is
hinted at in the *Portrait,* when Stephen conceives himself as "the
artist forging anew in his workshop out of the sluggish matter of
the earth a new soaring impalpable imperishable being" (196).
The being is of course "the uncreated conscience" of his race
(299), the Pseudo-Dionysius' uncreated Creator, Aristotle's unmoved Mover; but there is an overtone of mockery in the passage, for it recalls the youthful Augustine and his evil companions, "desiring to be cleansed from these defilements, by carrying
food to those who were called 'elect' and 'holy,' out of which, in
the workhouse of their stomachs, they should forge for us Angels
and Gods, by whom we might be cleansed." [1] For Joyce the holy
ones are the artists, who create themselves as gods. In *Ulysses* the
blasphemy is carried further: Mr. Deasy, for example, hates the
Jews because, as he says, "they sinned against the light"—the

Notes to Chapter IV begin on page 148.

light that falls on him, as on Danae, like golden coins (34, 37)—
and Stephen, by smashing the light in the brothel (567–568),
identifies himself with the Jews. Here again, however, it is against
materialism that he rebels: he smashes the light not because it is
a light but because it is part of the equipment of a brothel.
Throughout *Ulysses* and its predecessors, Joyce is like those
saints whose reckless piety offends the prescriptions and proscrip-
tions of orthodoxy; with *Finnegans Wake* he disavows piety also.
As an artist, after a long struggle to become godlike by refining
himself out of existence, he accepts the judgment of Justius—
"anarch, egoarch" (188)—and identifies himself with the first
outcast. As a symptom of the atmosphere of our time this is as
dubious as it is obvious; as an indication of Joyce's impiety it
should be sufficient answer to those critics who would make him
an unaffiliated Christian, a moralist in any accepted sense of the
term, or even a disinterested artist.

His conception of Cain as a suffering titan and Abel as a belly-
patting philistine parallels that of Baudelaire in "Abel et Caïn";
but Joyce is humorous where Baudelaire is merely bitter. Joyce
has mastered the pain of apostasy enough to make use of it
through pity and laughter alike. This sounds sentimental, but
I know of no more accurate words. Shem frankly calls himself
"Pariah, cannibal Cain" (193), and mocks his brother: "I cain
but are you able?" (287). Shaun, "Immaculatus, . . . Altrues,
. . . a chum of the angelets, . . . that mothersmothered model,
that goodlooker without a flaw whose spiritual toilettes were the
talk of half the town" (191), is a "heavybuilt Abelbody" (63),
"raumybult and abelboobied" (416); he rightly suspects that
Shem's book (which he thumbs through in a few seconds) is "all
about crime and libel" (419), and accordingly threatens to "do
a whisper drive" (193) against the author:

> For there's no true spell in Connacht or hell
> (bis) That's able to raise a Cain (47).[2]

This romantic conception, developed by Gessner, Byron and
others, Joyce modified and strengthened by blending with it the
orthodox Catholic view. This is not to say that he was orthodox

in any sense, but that his unorthodoxy was grounded in a sure
knowledge of the doctrines he disavowed and a not unsympa-
thetic understanding of the attitudes he opposed. Saint Anselm,
for example, in his third and sixteenth meditations, laments the
sins of his youth in a way that Joyce can only have found
sympathetic:

> Alas! from what height have you fallen, to what depth have
> you plunged! Woe! what benignity have you contemned,
> what malignity have you embraced! What have you done,
> O conscious madness, mad foulness, foul wickedness, what
> have you done? . . . My God, where have I gone? where
> have I fled? where have I hidden? Cast out from before Thy
> face like Cain, I have lived a vagabond and a fugitive in the
> earth, and whoever finds me shall slay me! [3]

Anselm's life was similar in many ways to that of Joyce, his temperament had points of similarity, and his euphuistic rhetoric,
his capering logic and his emotional extravagance must have
appealed to the artist as a young man. But the appeal was
limited. Saint Anselm was no Shaun by any means; nevertheless,
he became Archbishop of Canterbury, a fighter for ecclesiastical
autonomy, and a champion of unreasoning orthodoxy: "If one
can understand [the faith] rationally, let him thank God; if he
can't, let him not boast of his strength, brandishing his horns,
but bow his head in reverence." [4] To that way of life Joyce
brought, as he said, "the spirit of an acute sympathetic alien." [5]
Having experienced sin, fear and trembling, repentance, for-
giveness, grace and amendment, he deliberately rejected that
way of life.[6] Like the young Moses in *Ulysses,* he would not bow
his head or bow his will (141). But his artist's pride did not
preclude—rather it required—the most ruthless self-knowledge.
His unorthodoxy therefore was not of any traditional kind. He
was not a thoroughgoing Promethean. As Justius justly observed
in *Finnegans Wake,* Mercius was "of twosome twiminds forenenst
gods, hidden and discovered"; his kingdom was "disunited," his
soul vacuous and "most intensely doubtful" (188). It was his
insistence on the open mind, on the right to leave questions un-

answered rather than accept official answers, that offended both
religion and society. This attitude, rather than any body of doctrine, was his heresy. It is a homelessness both willful and wistful.
The conversations of the Mookse and the Gripes, the Ondt and
the Gracehoper, and Justius and Mercius (unlike those of Hermes
and Prometheus, Megaera and Tantalus, Uriel and Satan, the
bee and the spider, and other messengers and exiles, which they
superficially resemble) show that Shem never quite managed to
shake off the burden of guilt laid on him by public opinion—
which is to say that to some extent he sympathized with Shaun's
view. As a person of insight, and as an artist using the most social
of all media, language, he could not very well do otherwise.
Though he sardonically calls the bland Burrus "A king off duty
and a jaw forever" (162), he admits (with a stammer because of
the moses in his sole [167]) that Caseous stinks: "Cheesugh! you
complain. And Hi Hi High must say you are not Hoa Hoa
Hoally in the wrong!" (163).[7] This is the burden of Joyce's
medieval training; it informs not only the specific references
to Cain and Abel but all passages dealing with Shem and Shaun
under whatever names. The references to Cain and Abel in
Migne's indices to the Latin fathers direct us (without turning
us pale) to many orthodox commentaries; a few examples will
suffice to show how closely Joyce follows the line—and to what
an unorthodox end. It is the unorthodoxy of God before the
Grand Inquisitor, but it is also the admitted wickedness of Cain.

The death of Abel, according to all orthodox interpreters,
prefigures the death of Christ; Abel accordingly is the archetype
of the Christians and Cain of the Jews; [8] Abel, of all good,[9]
just,[10] innocent [11] and humble [12] men, of the Christian martyrs,[13]
and of the church; [14] Cain, of all wicked, proud, unjust, impatient
men, of heretics,[15] and of those who are concerned with this world
rather than the next.[16] Saint Ambrose sums up the position:

> Under the names of the two brothers, two types of people,
> two contrary ways of life contend with each other. Those
> of one party believe that their own minds are the authors
> of all reason, all meaning, and all suggestion; that is to say,
> they ascribe all discoveries and inventions to human inge-

nuity. Those of the other party defer to God, creator and mover of all things, and submit in all things to the governance of their divine parent and guide. The former are signified by Cain, the latter by Abel. These two types were created by one spirit, conceived in one womb, and born as brothers; but they are contraries, since they were born with different and antagonistic minds. Assuredly such enemies can never live as one family.[17]

Cain was of course the founder of the first city, and his descendants were the first inventors and discoverers (Genesis 4:17–22). The Eternal City also was founded by a fratricide. In fact, says Saint Augustine, the City of Man is at war with the City of God; [18] Isidore, Bishop of Seville, says, "Enoch, son of Cain, in whose name his father founded the city, signifies the impious who are given to this life"; [19] and Rupert, Abbot of Tuitium, concluding his commentary on the story, says,

> Lastly, it is to be noted that the occasion for building the first earthly city was homicide. For Cain had killed his brother and had thus become hateful to all, a vagabond and a fugitive in the earth; therefore he built a city where he might take refuge, having turned away from the face of God and having no share in His celestial city.[20]

It may be that the fratricide offers mankind the gifts of civilization, as Erich Fromm has maintained, by way of expiating a sense of guilt; [21] in any case, anti-urbanism seems to be universal. God made the country, we sing, man made the town. Abraham distrusted cities, and Lot fled them to save his innocence, though there is probably a moral of a different kind in the fact that after he reached the country (as my former student Charles Mann says) he lived the life of an Erskine Caldwell character. But we tend to forgive him (1) because he didn't know what he was doing and (2) because after all it was the only practical thing to do. The root of all evil is consciousness, intelligence, deliberate choice, the exercise of which is essentially an act of usurpation or at least an expression of dissatisfaction with the

divine arrangements. This was the basic vice of Cain, which he
inherited from his parents.[22] Adam was not content with Paradise.[23] In the most innocent of all possible worlds, he perversely
sought moral insight; as long as the Garden afforded none it did
not meet his requirements, because in the state of innocence he
himself did not meet his requirements. Innocence and insight
come from within, and he who will have one must forgo the
other. This is the native quirk of our species. The original sin
was intellectual curiosity, the quality that set Adam apart from
the other animals. It alienated him from nature, which asks no
questions and tells itself no lies. The peculiarly human quality
is inherently sinful: to be fully human is to be cast out from
grace. The glory of God is manifest in the physical grace of animals; man's alienation shows in his very walk, and whatever inward grace or glory he may achieve by intense thought is not
apparent to the rest of nature. In lonely madness he struggles
inwardly to create his own soul. This is the hell into which, of
his own free will, the creative spirit plunges from the Garden.
His wisdom is the devil's wisdom. The first individualist was
the Light-Bearer; it was inevitable that he should become the
Enemy. The theoretical physicist, the creative philosopher or
philologist, we regard with superstitious awe, and laugh away
our fear by calling them eggheads or longhairs. (In the dull
lexicon of retardation the terms are synonymous.) We feel instinctively that they are unsound. We itch to investigate their
un-American activities. They are Shem, the Enemy. But we rush
to buy the books of the inspirational "philosopher" and the
prestige-vending "grammarian," and for the engineer who ap-
plies physical theory we compete with display ads in *The New
York Times*. We feel instinctively that they are sound. They
are Shaun, the People's Friend.

Joyce is for the Enemy, who is after all our only real friend.
Shem, having been toed and shoe'd off the gorgeous premises of
all respectable people, even in the Land of Nod (181), excommunicated (173, 181) and "self-exiled in upon his ego" (184),
moaning like Cain "that his pawdry's purgatory was more than
a nigger bloke could bear" (177), shuts himself up in his house
O'Shame and plagiarizes the Pelagian heresy by the dancing light

phantastic of his gnose's luciferous glow (182). He freely admits
that he is dirty, smelly, unsocial and generally undesirable, and
that he envies Shaun's popularity. So much for orthodoxy. But
this is private self-knowledge, not conventional confession to an
authorized minister of grace. Practically all the medieval com-
mentators call Abel "just" and Cain "envious," [24] and several
assert that the fratricide compounded his sin by not confessing
it when God gave him the opportunity.[25] In *Finnegans Wake*,
Justius (a public virtue) accuses Mercius (a private virtue) of
having killed his "ittle brupper" (Justius) because of envy and
also "to see how his innards worked" (191).[26] He advises Mercius
to hide and invites him to confess (188), but Mercius, ignoring
the accusation, the invitation and the advice, communes with
himself to see how his own innards work. Justius is not only un-
merciful but unjust; but Mercius is certainly unsocial.

The brothers "are in such transfusion," Joyce admits, that it
is hard to tell "who is artthoudux from whose heterotropic"
(252),[27] but one thing neither he nor Shem will ever admit is
that Shaun is qualified to give intellectual or moral guidance.
Animal charm is not enough. "Poor, good, true, Jaun," sigh the
Leapyear Girls (431); but all his claims are false; he lacks every
quality ascribed to Abel. In the person of the Mookse he is an
authoritarian who can conceive of no human relationship but
that of domination and submission; the heretical Gripes is much
more charitable. In full Papal panoply the Mookse goes for a
walk in the woods, believing himself to be a god; like the
mercenary Xenophon, parsec for parasang, he marches to the
river of life, whose muddiness he tries to stare away. He answers the Gripes' polite greeting with arrogant rudeness and
threatens to turn him over to the secular arm for the *peine forte
et dure* (152-155). The Gripes' tragedy is that he can neither
deny the Mookse's emotional appeal nor surrender his own intellectual independence. To the Mookse's demand, "Will you
give you up?" he replies with humanistic equivocation: "If I con-
now make my submission, I cannos give you up" (154). This is
much too subtle for the Mookse. All the understanding, and all
the self-respect too, are on the side of the defeated Gripes.

When the amenities require it, however, the Abel type pre-

tends humility: "How all too unwordy am I, a mere mailman
of peace," says Shaun. A mailman is a messenger or angel; but
the Word is God. Shaun, protesting his submission, tells more
truth than he knows. His humility rings false in every article.
He pretends to be fond of Shem, with whom, he suggests, he once
lived in a relationship like that of Beaumont and Fletcher: "I'm
an everdevoting fiend of his. . . . I ought not to laugh with him
on this stage. But he' such a game loser! I lift my disk to him"
(408).[28] Nonetheless, Chuff warns the Leapyear Girls not to
harbor the outcast Glugg: "Though down to your dowerstrip
he's bent to knee he maunt know ledgings here" (233). The
girls are completely taken in by "the just one, their darling"
(470): "Dear Shaun," they call him, "good boy," "salve a tour,"
"honest Shaun," "Shaun honey," "dear Dogmestic Shaun,"
"frank Shaun," "kind Shaun," "Shaun illustrious," "thrice truth-
ful teller, Shaun of grace," "strong Shaun O'," "ingenious
Shaun," and "able Shaun" (409–413, 421–427). Nevertheless he
falls asleep in the middle of his after-dinner speech (426). Our
wide-awake author calls him "Pure Yawn" (474).

But Joyce's unorthodoxy and impiety are most unmistakable
in the Feeble of the Ondt and the Gracehoper, where the implications of Shaun's Freudian slip, "fiend" for "friend," are developed. "Ondt," as Tindall has pointed out, is Danish for "evil," [29]
and the Ondt's *haine* reaches to Heaven (416). This is devilish;
however, since he is raumybult and abelboobied (in much the
same way as the Emperor of Lilliput), it may be assumed that
he stands for Abel, and the vagabond Gracehoper for Cain. The
Ondt lolls on his lazy throne, "sated before his comfortumble
phullupsuppy of a plate o'monkynous and a confucion of minthe
(for he was a conformed aceticist and aristotaller)" (417). The
silver plate of monkeynuts turns out to be Platonic-monkish
nous or early medieval Christian Neo-Platonism; "minthe" is
the Greek *Minthē*, paramour of Hades, who according to one
version of her story was a rival of Persephone and according to
another version was Persephone herself. In the first version,
Hades rescued her from a beating at the hands of his jealous
wife by turning her into a plant, mint, which the Greeks believed
to be an aphrodisiac; in the second version Persephone was said

to stay in the underworld not by constraint but by choice, being
under a spell of love, and to return to the world reluctantly in
the form of the hot little herb. Gruppe says of this and other
aphrodisiacs, "These plants were regarded as the home of the
demon who kindles the fire of love." [30] Commenting on this
identification of love with death, Arthur Bernard Cook says,

> The Greeks of old aspired to an actual marriage-union with
> the deities of the underworld. . . . Every man would one
> day enter the bridal chamber of Persephone, every woman
> that of Hades. . . . In the embrace of Persephone the dead
> man becomes the chthonian king. Borne off by Hades the
> dead woman becomes the chthonian queen.

Such beliefs were of course the heart of the mystery cults, and
their medieval Christian analogue was expressed in such poems
as "Quia Amore Langueo" and Thomas Hales' "A Luve Ron."
But not until Joyce did anyone identify the Christian God with
Hades. The Ondt claims also to be a sour ascetic and a teetotal
Aristotelian. Here is confusion indeed!—for as Cook points out,
"Aristotle denied the possibility of love (*philía*) between man
and God." [31] He also denied the value of asceticism.[32] The last
confusion in this phullupsuppical hash is the decorous human-
ism of Confucius, whose nearest analogue in medieval Christen-
dom was probably John of Salisbury.

So much for the Ondt's qualification for intellectual leadership. As the Gracehoper observes, he occupies a lot of space but
he can't beat time. He is as little qualified for moral leadership.
His anthem is *Ad majorem l.s.d.! Divi gloriam;* his pounds, shil-
lings and pence are an anagram of *Laus Deo semper;* he cordially
invites the starving Gracehoper to partake of his *largesse*—that
is, of his greatness, his wisdom, and his pasture ("mine wide-
height")—and laughs until he almost chokes at his own wit. The
weeping Gracehoper forgives him, explains to him the meaning
of their relationship, and wishes him well. Again, all the faith,
hope, charity and understanding are with Cain. The fact that
Abel recites a fable so discreditable to himself indicates clearly
that he doesn't understand it (416). But it is his role to deliver
messages he doesn't understand.

In *Finnegans Wake*, Abel is always the aggressor and Cain the
victim. Glugg, "the bold bad bleak boy of the storybooks, who,
. . . because he knew to mutch, has been divorced into disgrace
court," makes naughty overtures to the Rainbow Girls: "Beamy
owen and calmy hugh and if you what you my call for me I will
wishyoumaycull for you"; his brother Chuff, "the fine frank fair-
haired fellow of the fairytales," whose "soard fleshed light like
likening," puts a stop to it, and Glugg, like Saint Cyprian's Abel,
meekly submits: "Arrest thee, scaldbrother! came the evangelion,
sabre accusant, from all Saint Joan's Wood to kill or maim him,
and be dumm but ill s'arrested. Et would proffer to his delected
one the his trifle from the grass" (219–223). The allusions in this
scene are unmistakably heretical in their drift. Hugh and Owen
Roe O'Neill were the most notable fighters for Irish independence in Elizabeth's time; with their deaths, the resistance col-
lapsed. Owen is said to have died from the prick of a poisoned
nail deliberately placed in his shoe; Hugh died an exile in Rome,
warmly welcomed by the Pope but in his last years blind.[33] The
devilish Glugg is recommending himself to the girls as an Abel-
bodied leader, a Catholic martyr, and a gentleman. The evangelion is evidently from a French account of Joan of Arc. I have
not found an exact parallel, but Chapelain's *La Pucelle* narrates
a number of similar encounters, for example, in Cantos III, X
and XII; and Voltaire's parody, *La Pucelle d'Orléans*, is full of
them. Saint Joan's Wood is mentioned in the official record of
the trial of Saint Joan:

> There is also a wood, called the oak-wood, . . . which can
> be seen from her father's door; . . . she has heard from her
> brother that in the country around it is said she received
> her message at the tree; but she says she did not, and told
> him quite the contrary.[34]

After such an explicit denial, the fact that Chuff comes from the
wood shows what a false little angel he is. His sword makes the
light of Heaven a killer, for "likening" is a mirror, which in
folk belief is widely regarded as an instrument of death.[35] Glugg
meets this threat by offering him "the his trifle from the grass,"

leçon trufe de la grâce, a trifling lesson in grace—to wit, a truffle,
which in Old French was a trifle, and which in the sixteenth century, according to a quotation in the *New English Dictionary,*
was believed to "haue power of Chastity, and to subdue the
flesh." This is mockery, and not pious mockery. There can be no
doubt that in *Finnegans Wake* Joyce is on the side of the devils.
His use of the materials of orthodoxy should not be miscon-
strued. He uses them in much the same way that Marx uses
Hegel and the devil quotes Scripture.

CHAPTER V

The Transfused Brothers: Jacob and Esau

"The mythologists seem to agree with some thinkers of the present day, who . . . say that both the good and the beautiful appear in the nature of things only when that nature has made some progress."—Aristotle, *Metaphysics*, XIV, 4.

THE FIRST TWO PAGES OF *Finnegans Wake*, IN WHICH ALL THE themes of the novel are announced,[1] include two references to the deception—or apparent deception—of "bland old Isaac." This is one of the more difficult themes, for it involves the relations of Jacob and Esau, who, like those primitive vaudevillians Mutt and Jute, "swop hats" until they are all but indistinguishable. In the universe of H. C. Earwicker, as in that of Heraclitus, everything flows, and the search for clear-cut patterns is liable to be stultifying; this is not to say that the flow is chaotic or to deny what Joyce asserted, that there are motifs and recurrences; it is only to recognize the fluidity of the patterns and the tendency of opposites to "reamalgamerge." This is particularly necessary with regard to Jacob and Esau, in treating whom Joyce seems—but only seems—to be inconsistent.

For Joyce's sympathy is not with the exile, the outcast and the "downandoutermost" as such, but with the independent thinker. He has much more respect for Professor MacHugh than for Kevin Egan, Lenehan, Gumley, or the grotesques of Nighttown. Even less than Shaun is Shem a "helotwashipper." The Joycean

Notes to Chapter V begin on page 152.

hero, though his ends are not those of the world, is not above
the shifts of wordly wisdom as means. There is enough of the
Jesuit in Joyce for him to believe that in some cases the best of
ends may not be corrupted by the worst of means. "Ex nickylow
malo comes mickelmassed bonum" (23).[2] In the case of Jacob
and Esau, Joyce's attitude toward winner and loser is the opposite of that he takes in the cases of the Mookse and the Gripes,
the Ondt and the Gracehoper, Justius and Mercius, Chuff and
Glugg, and the other manifestations of Shem and Shaun. Joyce
is for the independent thinker when he wins, no less than when
he loses—and through Jacob, as we shall see, all such losers win
out in the end. The moral of the Bible story is a Joycean moral:
that any means employed to win the blessing of God are godly,
no matter how unsocial or unbrotherly they may be.[3] The main
thing is to value the blessing, which is to have a capacity for it.
Esau's sin is that he druther eat; and bland old Isaac himself,
who though blind is neither deaf nor stupid, can make a plausi-
ble pretense of being deceived through satisfaction of the body's
hunger.[4] The body's hunger, which betrayed even Joyce into
sentimental exaggeration,[5] is Shaun's chief motive, as it was
Esau's; the desire to be undeceived is Shem's, as it was Jacob's;
"Shem is as short for Shemus as Jem is joky for Jacob" (169),
and Shaun, we shall see, is several times identified as Esau.

The world instinctively prefers Esau, whose simple motive is
easy to understand and whose obvious misfortune is easy to
sympathize with. The man who wrestles with God is suspect,
even though he prevail—or because he prevails. We never forgive him his limp or his secret. Although, like the Hilary who
became a tristian and the Tristopher who became a playboy
(21–22),[6] the brothers are "in such transfusion" that it is hard to
tell "who is artthoudux from whose heterotropic" (252), there
are discernible and characteristic differences between them. They
are as different as hay and straw. "What true feeling for their's
hayair with what strawng voice of false jiccup!" (4). Isaac does
have a true feeling for the heir's hair and smell of hay; he is
not deceived; with a strong voice, affecting a hiccup, he blesses
the false Jacob, the true heir. So does Joyce.

But the matter is complicated by the fact that Joyce had read the commentaries as well as the text; for the orthodox commentaries involved a view of the church which Joyce could not accept; though consistent within themselves, they included elements to which Joyce found it difficult to respond consistently. He solved the problem by having Jacob and Essau amalgamerge.

His response to the thinker in Jacob and the philistine in Esau is quite orthodox. At the outset of his career Joyce had asserted that an artist who courts the favor of the multitude is liable to become infected with its timidity and obligated to its sodden enthusiasm: "his true servitude is that he inherits a will broken by doubt." [7] The young man who wrote this might himself have written the passage in which Saint Ambrose explains the prophecy, "The elder shall serve the younger," and justifies the events of Genesis 25–27, on the grounds of Esau's servile nature and Jacob's wisdom:

> Everyone serves who lacks the authority of a pure conscience. Everyone serves who is broken by fear, or bound by delight, or led by greed, or made savage by anger, or cast down by sorrow. For all passion is servile; therefore he who sins is a slave to sin, and, what is worse, a slave to many masters: he who is subject to vices has delivered himself up to many masters, and will hardly be released from slavery to them. But he who is master of his will, judge of his motives and interpreter of his judgments, who subdues the appetites of bodily passion and does well whatever he does, in doing well does rightly; and he who does rightly is guiltless and blameless, since he has power over his acts: he is indeed free. [8]

Thus far Joyce follows Ambrose, agreeing also with Augustine's interpretation, "Esau represents carnal, Jacob spiritual men." [9] In fact, the relations of HCE, ALP, Shaun and Shem are strikingly similar to those of Issac, Rebecca, Esau and Jacob. On matters of human behavior, Joyce frequently agrees with the theologians; thus, according to Saint Augustine, Esau and Jacob prefigured respectively the wicked and the good even in the bosom of the church. Just as the brothers came from one seed of Isaac,

> . . . so from one Baptism of our Lord Savior and from the womb of one Church were born the Christian nation, who by difference of morals are divided like Esau and Jacob into two parties; and by the fruits of their labors one party is known as carnal, the other as spiritual. For this reason God said, "The greater shall serve the lesser," for the number of the wicked is always greater than that of the good. And as those two infants in the womb of Rebecca, even so are these two nations in the body of the Church until they shall be brought together on the Day of Judgment. Until that time, . . . the humble will be fought by the proud, the chaste will be pursued by the adulterous, the sober will be derided by the drunken (whose number is countless), the kind will be attacked by the jealous and the generous by the rapacious, the wrathful will lust to exterminate the peaceful, and those who have a taste for heavenly things will be urged by the voluptuous to come down to earth.[10]

This might be part of an account of *Finnegans Wake,* so close is it to Joyce's theme. But Joyce cannot proceed to the next step of the argument, which is that the senescence of Isaac prefigures the obsolescence of the Old Testament with its message of earthly hope for the first people of God; that Esau prefigures the Jews, Jacob the Christians (the second people of God), and Rebecca the church.[11] This last point especially he cannot accept, for one of his cardinal beliefs is that the church is not a friend but an enemy of spiritual life. Roma, he says, is a poor imitation of Amor (487). The low metaphor of Father Purdon in "Grace"; the contrast, in the *Portrait,* between Stephen's vision of "wild creatures racing, their feet pattering like rain upon the leaves," and the reality of the "heavily shod feet" and "uncouth faces" of "a squad of Christian Brothers . . . on its [not *their*] way back from the Bull" (192)—for all the world like the squad of constables in *Ulysses* (160)—the genial grossness of Father Conmee and the brutality of the Mookse indicate the persistence of Joyce's conviction that the church was not spiritual but anti-spiritual. The brother who stands for the church in *Finnegans Wake* is Esau, not Jacob. However, as I have indicated in Chapter IV, the mature Joyce rejected the spiritual as well as the political and social aspects of Christianity; this rejection complicates his treatment of Jacob and Esau, as we shall see later; but first it is necessary to show the reversal of traditional roles.

According to all orthodox interpreters, Jacob prefigures Christ; thus, Zeno, Bishop of Verona, says, "Jacob was the image of Christ"; [12] and Augustine says, "We have frequently suggested to your charity, dearest brothers, that the blessed Jacob was the type and figure of our Lord Savior." [13] But in *Finnegans Wake* the Esau figures are addressed as "Salve a tour" (409) and hold the office of Pope (152), whereas the Jacob figures are accused of impiety (188), excommunicated (172), and identified with the devil (222–223). For Joyce, Esau was the type of the natural man, Jacob of the civilized man; from this essential difference flow all their particular differences. Of course no man is merely civilized; nor, insofar as he is a man and not a simpler animal, merely natural. The difference is one of emphasis and tendency; but it is plain enough, and Joyce, while recognizing that it is not absolute, dramatizes its significance. His natural man is hairy, sleepy, hungry for natural foods, impulsive and given to direct action, but withal hypocritical because he understands nothing, least of all himself; the civilized man is smooth, wakeful, hungry for canned foods, introspective, and given to doubt, irony, exile, silence and cunning, but withal honest because, though others may betray him, he never deceives himself. Both are subject to sexual temptation; Glugg openly tries to seduce the Rainbow Girls (223), but Shaun preaches the Leapyear Girls a sermon on chastity, full of Freudian *double-entendres* reeking with perversion (434ff.). Joyce, viewing both brothers from a distance, calls them "Jerkoff and Eatsoup" (246).

Shaun is the very picture of a primitive (405), a blue-toothed Teuton with a horny hide and the beak of a wild Indian, who suggests Jugurtha though he can't pronounce the name (403). He describes himself as "like the regular redshank" (primitive

Celt), "impregnable as the mule" (411)—in unwitting recognition of his sterility and his homosexual tendencies. He has as little taste as Esau for the responsibilities of civil life. He druther eat; he lives, like Esau, in the fatness of the earth and the dew of Heaven (Genesis 27:39); food, sex and religion, in fact, are almost all he thinks about, and that suits his public fine. His tabernacle, like theirs, is a tablenapkin. When he arrives on the scene the Leapyear Girls sigh, "May the turtle's blessings of God and Mary and Haggispatric and Huggisbrigid be souptumbling all over him!" (404). He replies, "Lard have mustard on them!" (405). Immediately, "in the sighed of lovely eyes while his knives of hearts made havoc he had recruited his strength by meals of spadefuls of mounded food, in anticipation of the faste of the tablenapkins," uttering prayers and singing like Faust, "Margareta, Candy Eater!" between mouthfuls. This is all he does for four days (405–407). When he rises to speak he hiccups, belches and can hardly keep awake, what with "anteproprevious-day's pigeons-in-a-pie with rough dough . . . and the hash-say-ugh of overgestern pluzz the 'stuesday's shampain in his head, with the memories of the past and the hicnuncs of the present embelliching the musics of the futures from Miccheruni's band" (407). Nevertheless, the Leapyear Girls welcome his "stewed letters" and hope he has been appointed their savior. He begins speaking "with a good catlick tug at his cocomoss candylock, a foretaste in time of his cabbageous brain's curlyflower" (409). As modestly and truthfully as his limited intelligence will permit, he tells them that he has indeed been appointed to save them, though he didn't and doesn't want the job: "Not what I wants to do a strike of work but it was condemned on me . . . by Hireark Books and Chiefoverseer Cooks . . . and there does be a power coming over me from on high out of the book of breedings" [Genesis]; since "it is becoming hairydittary," he has "of coerce" nothing to look forward to but killing time (409–410). He could think of more congenial ways to kill it; he would like to bury himself in his cool wine cellar, the wine-dark sea: "deep in my wineupon ponteen." As for giving them spiritual guidance, "I am hopeless off course to be doing anything concerning" (410). The only use he has for monasticism, he tells them, is to get outside it—that is, to eat it; the only blessing he knows is "For quid we have recipimus, recipe, O lout!" and among his most characteristic proverbs are "Mass and meat mar no man's journey. Eat a missal lest" (456).

But the girls have heard that he will bring them news of salvation, and they beg him to tell them about the enameled surface of the faith. As to that, he replies, he can do it—but with characteristic slackness he stops in the middle of the opening phrase to pick his teeth: "As, Shaun replied patly, with tootle-pick tact too and a down of his dampers, to that I have the gum-power" (410). His explanation is that he intends to work as little as possible and sleep as much as possible, but withal to subscribe to the correct doctrines and recite the daily *gratia bene's* for the sake of his daily bread and broth, like a good dog. He concludes with the exclamatory "Credo!" of Cardinal MacHale, referred to in "Grace," and offers his hand and tongue: the protruding tongue of mockery, the eloquent tongue of rhetoric, and the grateful tongue of a dog. The whole speech is an act of worship, Shaun's God being his belly: "I can now truthfully declaret . . . that I do my reasonabler's best to recite my grocery beans. . . . Ghee [butter] up, ye dog, for your daggily broth, etc., Happy Maria and Glorious Patrick, etc., etc. In fact, always, have I believe. Greedo! Her's me hongue!" (411). During the sermon that follows he pauses to refresh himself, "taking at the same time, as his hunger got the bitter of him, a hearty bite out of the honeycomb of his . . . Melosedible hat" (422), and says apropos of nothing, "By the bun, is it you goes bisbuiting His Esaus and Cos and then throws them bag in the box? Why the tin's nearly empty" (433).

This gastric obsession is a characteristic of all the Esau figures in *Finnegans Wake*. Thus, Jute (Esau) says to Mutt (Jacob), "You that side your voise are almost inedible to me" (16). Of the three meanings in this sentence, two are metaphors of eating: (1) You on that side—your voice is almost inaudible to me. (2) You on that side—I can hardly stomach your ways. (3) I can hardly stomach you who speak out of the side of your mouth. (Shem did speak out of the side of his mouth [173].) When Jute swears, he says, "Boildoyle and rawhoney on me"; when he means to say "barely," it comes out "beuraly" (butterly), and for "good afternoon" he says, "Gut aftermeal" (17). The Ondt, the hero of his own "grimm gest of Jacko and Esaup" (414), is shown "sated before his comfortumble phullupsuppy" (417), and the Leapyear Girls dream of their future life with Shaun, Kevin, Dolph and Chuff as a perpetual feast of sweets:

> T will be waiting for uns. . . . Our cousin gourmand, Percy, the pup, will denounce the sniffnomers of all callers. . . . Lady Marmela Shortbred will walk in for supper with her marchpane switch on, her necklace of almonds and her poirette Sundae dress with bracelets of honey and her cochineal hose with the caramel dancings, . . . and her suckingstaff of ivorymint. . . . And the Prince Le Monade has been graciously pleased. His six chocolate pages will run bugling before him and Cococream toddle after with his sticksword in a pink cushion (235–236).

All these and all such are born to consume. The multitude feeds them because it loves them because it feeds them. But he who feeds the multitude does so at his peril, unless he puts himself on their level by charging the highest price the traffic will bear. For the sake of their self-esteem the multitude cannot permit the genuine superiority of one who gives with no ulterior motive; they will submit to tyranny but not to disinterestedness or benevolence. With a true instinct of collective self-preservation the multitude destroys the man whose ways are better than its ways, whose motives it admires but does not quite believe in; and it finds more acceptable motives for doing good: "It is more blessed to give than to receive" (Acts 20:35). "If thine enemy hunger, feed him; if he thirst, give him drink; for in so doing thou shalt heap coals of fire on his head" (Romans 12:20). The Christian religion is largely devoted to celebrating the crucifixion of the benevolent man, both from his own point of view and from that of the multitude; its sentimental-cynical insight is unparalleled.

Shem incurs the hatred of the multitude not only because he declines to participate in popular movements—because, as Shaun tells him, "you . . . sleep at our vigil and fast for our feast" (189)—and the word "for" suggests that Shem went hungry to provide the feast—but because, like Jacob, he is more interested in cooking than in eating. This is something the multitude cannot understand. They enjoy the product but scorn the process, and through Shaun's *vox populi* they mock their disinterested artist of a cook:

> It never stphruck your mudhead's obtundity . . . that the more carrots you chop, the more turnips you slit, the more murphies you peel, the more onions you cry over, the more bullbeef you butch, the more mutton you crackerhack, the more potherbs you pound, the fiercer the fire and the longer your spoon and the harder you gruel with more grease to your elbow the merrier fumes your new Irish stew (190).

When Shem does eat, his unnatural taste offends all right-thinking people: he prefers canned salmon to fresh and canned pineapple to junglegrown, and the low sham has no taste at all for what honest men enjoy:

> None of your inchthick blueblooded Balaclava fried-at-belief-stakes or juicejelly legs of the Grex's molten mutton or greasilygristly grunters' goupons or slice upon slab of luscious goosebosom with lump after load of plumpudding stuffing all aswim in a swamp of bogoakgravy for that greekenhearted yudel Rosbif of Old Zealand! he could not attouch it (170–171).

There is the same difference between "nicechild Kevin," who "irishsmiled in his milky way of cream dwibble and onage tustard and dessed tabbage," and "badbrat Jerry," who "furrinfrowned down his wrinkly waste of methylated spirits, ick, and lemoncholy lees, ick, and pulverised rhubarbarorum, icky"; (555).

Here we have an amalgamerging of the blessed Jacob with the cursed Cain—for were they not both types of the artist? Jacob "sod pottage" (Genesis 25:29); Cain built the first city (Genesis 4:17); Shem "sod town" (224). The artist is both blessed

and cursed by his power of evocation, as Plato explicitly recognized;[14] the thinker is both blessed and crippled by his insight.
Jacob's limp is analogous to the sign of Cain, which we are told
was a trembling of the limbs and a habit of moaning.[15] But this
directly opposes the orthodox view, which is that Esau is analogous to Cain, and Jacob to Abel; that Rebecca, like Eve, "produced two principles of human nature, one of good, the other
of evil. . . . (Esau was the type of evil, Jacob showed forth the
figure of good)." [16]

There is really no inconsistency here, for orthodoxy maintains
that what is good in the sight of the world is evil in the sight of
God. So far Joyce is perfectly orthodox: his view of the relative
merits of Jacob and Esau coincides exactly with that of the
fathers. Where he differs from them is in his view of the church.
In modern Ireland, Stephen Dedalus said, "Caesar confesses
Christ and Christ confesses Caesar that together they may wax
fat"; [17] under such conditions the spiritual man finds himself outside the church and opposed to it.

But in *Finnegans Wake* Joyce disavows spirituality also: Jacob
for him is as bad as Esau, though in a different way. Are they
"two dreamyums in one dromium? Yes and no error. And both
as like as a duel of lentils? Peacisely" (89). Shem scorns his birth-
right, "Irrland's split little pea," in favor of "the hash of lentils
in Europe" (171). One of the Four Masters, trying to find out
which of the brothers wrote the book Shaun claims to have written, says, "The gist is the gist of Shaun but the hand is the hand
of Sameas" (483). He has a true insight, since one of the leading
motifs of the book is "the coincidance of their contraries" (49);
but Shaun, whose nature forbids him to understand their relationship, denies it in the words of Cain: "Nwo, nwo! This bolt
in hand be my worder! . . . What cans such wretch to say to I
or how have My to doom with him? We were wombful of mis-
chief and initiumwise, everliking a liked, hairytop on heeltipper,
. . . an ikeson am ikeson. . . . Been Ike hins kindergardien?"
(483). But the Old Master, unconvinced, replies with a medieval
proverb and the words of Ike himself: "Hood maketh not frere.[18]
The voice is the voice of jokeup, I fear" (487). To this the confused Shaun replies in the manner of the Alsatian proverb of

1870—*"Français ne peux, Allemand ne veux, Alsacien suis"*—
"Same no can, home no will, gangin I am. Gangang is Mine and
I will return" (487). Thus he unwittingly acknowledges the truth
of the exiled Shem's contention that the brothers are interde-
pendent and in essence one.

What Shem's superior knowledge amounts to is a recognition
that there is something of Shaun in himself; and Shaun, unconsciously and against his will, after many scornful denials, admits
that there is something of Shem in himself. He claims, in fact,
to have given Shem his "idioglossary" (423), and says he may
himself some day write "the authordux Book of Lief" (425).
The afterthought, that he would never for anything take the
trouble to do it, because he is "altogether a chap too fly and
hairyman for to infradig the like of that ultravirulence" (425),
comes too late; it is pure Shaun, but the Shemian ambition, if
nothing else, has been admitted; in his dream the "adipose rex"
(499) identifies himself briefly with the primitive "Chorley guy,"
Mutt, or Shem (16); he tells Shem that even though they fight
there is really no reason why they can't be "as chummy as two
bashed spuds," greets him respectfully—"Fee gate has Heenan
hoity, mind uncle Hare?" (*Wie geht es ihnen heute, mein
dunkler Herr?*)—and tries to sell him a paper or a poss of porter-
pease (466). Thus he recognizes Shem's superior position in the
cosmos. Esau does want the blessing; his only difficulty is that
he wants the pottage too; and though when faced with the
necessity of making a choice he chooses the pottage every time,
he does regret the loss of the blessing. Issac's assurance that he
will have the fat of the earth and the dew of Heaven doesn't altogether console him.

This of course contradicts the orthodox belief that the brothers are irreconcilably opposed—a belief which Joyce attributes
to Esau, not to Jacob. Thus, Jacob, who (the Bible story being
reversed) haunts the guilty dreams of Esau, wins out in the end
because he is after all more realistic. There are inconsistencies
in the character of each; in revealing them Joyce has been consistent both artistically and with regard to his view of the church.
The exile is neither completely damned nor completely free;
nor is the stay-at-home completely at home with himself or the

values he lazily accepts. In every man there is something of the holy sinner, the perfect Christ burdened with all men's guilt.[19] God helps no man carry his pack, Joyce seems to say; but the creative man, to whatever extent he can, helps himself.

CHAPTER VI

Jesuit Bark and Bitter Bite:
Ignatius Loyola

"The most painful secrets of their conscience, all, all, they will
bring to us, and we shall have an answer for all. And they will
be glad to believe our answer, for it will save them from the
great anxiety and the terrible agony they endure at present in
making a free decision for themselves."—The Grand Inquisitor,
The Brothers Karamazov

THE JESUITS NEVER FORGAVE JOYCE FOR REFUSING TO ENTER THEIR
Society, and he never forgave them for inviting him. The influence of this quarrel on his career is well known, and the effects
of his Jesuit training on his work are often remarked in a general
way.[1] It remains, however, to specify the effects; for only when
they are specified can we see clearly just what he rebelled against
and why his rebellion took the forms it did. Joyce's books are in
fact full of echoes from those of Saint Ignatius Loyola; we might
begin by identifying some of them and assessing their significance.

In *Ulysses* Buck Mulligan always uses the term "jesuit" as a
synonym for "casuist," but then his mission in life is to misunderstand everything; and Stephen Dedalus, calling on Saint Ignatius
to help him seduce his listeners by the cheap and easy device of
local color (186) or "composition of place," [2] is merely mocking
his own education. For he knows well enough that the corner-
stone of Jesuitism is not intellectual trickery but intellectual
obedience; and this was what neither Stephen nor Joyce would
ever yield, whether to their classmates at school or to Christ's

Notes to Chapter VI begin on page 155.

viceroy on earth. Their adoption of Satan's motto was by way of reaction against their training in obedience; the reaction was violent because the training had begun to take effect, and Joyce's continued self-centeredness throughout his life is evidence of a continuing need to disobey an organization whose members re-nounce their selfhood. This in itself was a kind of victory for the Jesuits, since compulsive disobedience is a form of intellectual dependence. A person mature in freedom can obey or disobey as circumstances may warrant; he has no neurotic need to refuse all restraint, to defy all authority, or to boast, as Joyce did in *Finnegans Wake,* that the disorder of his living quarters is "quite puzzonal" (183). One does not come off uninjured from exposure to authoritarianism.

Though the Society of Jesus is hardly a mass movement, readers of Eric Hoffer's *The True Believer* will have no difficulty in understanding its appeal. What won the admiration and al-most the allegiance of the young Joyce was a society whose mem-bers give their superiors the unquestioning obedience of sol-diers,[3] not only outwardly but inwardly:

> Let holy Obedience, in execution, in will and in under-standing, be always most perfect in us; let us obey, with great promptness, and spiritual joy and perseverance, what-ever shall be commanded us, persuading ourselves that all commands are just, and giving up in blind obedience our own conflicting opinion or judgment; this applies to all things whatsoever commanded by the Superior, unless it can be shown (as has been said) that some kind of sin is in-volved. Let everyone persuade himself that those who live under Obedience must let themselves be led and ruled by divine providence through their Superiors, as a corpse would be, that lets itself be carried here and there and treated in any way, or like an old man's staff, that permits itself to be used anywhere and in any way that he who holds it wishes.[4]

As Joyce matured he found it increasingly difficult to admire his teachers, who lived under such discipline, for it seemed to him that by mortifying their wills they degraded themselves and damaged or destroyed their souls. Stephen Dedalus, in the *Portrait,* watches the dean of studies at University College:

> It seemed as if he used the shifts and lore and cunning of the
> world, as bidden to do, for the greater glory of God, without
> joy in their handling or hatred of that in them which was
> evil but turning them, with a firm gesture of obedience, back
> upon themselves: and for all this silent service it seemed as
> if he loved not at all the master and little, if at all, the ends
> he served. *Similiter atque senis baculus,* he was, as the
> founder would have had him, like a staff in an old man's
> hand, to be leaned on in the road at nightfall or in stress
> of weather, to lie with a lady's nosegay on a garden seat, to
> be raised in menace (217).

Such moral passivity, such disavowal of personal responsibility,
of course militated against the development of the artist; but before he knew what he wanted to do, it attracted him. As a child
he often thought of himself as "The Reverend Stephen Dedalus,
S.J." (182–187). The Jesuits' freedom from self, so deceptively
similar to the artist's ideal freedom from personal involvement
with the ideas and other materials he uses, inevitably appealed
to the unformed artist; but since it is not at all the same thing
as that freedom, he inevitably came to the appalling realization
that for him at least it would be disastrous. It appealed also because it presented an alternative of order to the disorder of the
child's home; for the artist, however, order must come from
within, and is not to be confused with suppression of the will
or abdication of the mind. In *Stephen Hero,* Dedalus "cursed"
the influence of Catholicism on Ireland, "an island . . . the in-
habitants of which entrust their wills and minds to others that
they may ensure for themselves a life of spiritual paralysis" (146).
Joyce's rebellion, like that of the Greek Daedalus, consisted in
escaping. To escape, he had to renounce his education; for the
Jesuits are primarily educators, and their schools, guided by
Ignatius' *Ratio Studiorum,** inculcate obedience to authority and

---

* Quotations numbered 5, 6, 7, 9, and 10 are by permission from *St.
Ignatius and the Ratio Studiorum,* ed. by Edward A. Fitzpatrick. Copyright,
1933. McGraw-Hill Book Company, Inc.

recognition of the degrees of authority. The Rector or chief ex-
ecutive of a college, for example, is admonished to observe his
own "subordination in obedience not only to the General [the
world head of the Society of Jesus] but also to the Provincial
[the national head]"; all others in the college, students, teachers,
administrative officials and menial servants alike, are admonished

> to reverence and respect in the highest degree their Rector
> as one who is a vice-regent of Christ the Lord, by leaving
> to him the free disposal of themselves and of all they have
> with true obedience; by keeping nothing barred from him,
> not even their own conscience, which they should open to
> him . . . on stated occasions, and oftener if the case de-
> mand. . . . By a thing barred is to be understood a closed
> door, a chest, etc.[5]

In such a school there is of course no question of academic
freedom. Each professor is told precisely how to present his subject. Thus, the professor of theology is warned that in discussing
any question, "It is not enough for him to state the opinions of
learned men and reserve his own: he shall either defend the
views of St. Thomas, . . . or omit the question entirely." [6] Research and writing are subject to the same kind of control; the
professor of philosophy, for example,

> shall not treat of the digressions of Averroes (and the same
> judgment holds for others of this kind) in any separate
> treatise, and if anything good is to be cited from him, let
> him bring it out without praise, and, if possible, let him
> show that he has taken it from some other source.[7]

This is in keeping with a general rule of the Society: "Different
doctrines are not to be admitted. . . . True union and mutual
conformity are to be most diligently fostered; nor are things
which oppose them to be permitted." [8]

Such restraints are inevitably reflected in the teachers' attitude
toward their students' work. In *Stephen Hero* we are told that
the president of the college is also the censor of the student

literary society, and that all papers intended for presentation to
the society must first be submitted to him for approval (89). He
condemns Stephen's theory of art without even considering
whether it may be valid or not:

> —You think my theory of art is a false one?
> —It certainly is not the theory of art which is respected
> in this college (91). . . . But I have been very interested in
> it. I am sure too that when your studies have brought you
> further afield you will be able to amend it so as to—fit in
> more with recognised facts (98).

In their personal relationships too, the students at Jesuit
schools are kept under strict surveillance insofar as the *Ratio
Studiorum* is followed. They are not allowed to go out alone or
in casual groups, but only "two by two," each with a "companion" chosen not by himself but by the Rector; [9] for the younger
boys the Prefect of Lower Studies must appoint in each class a
Censor, "or, if the name censor is too little pleasing, a Chief
Decurion or Praetor," who is to report to the Prefect any mis-
behavior or irregularity of procedure, "whether the master was
present or not"—so that he acts as a check on the teacher as
well as on the boys; and in order for the unhappy boy or little
stinker to be "respected" by his fellow pupils, "let him be honored with some privilege, and let him have the right, with the
approval of the master, of begging off some lighter penalties for
his fellow pupils." [10]

In the *Portrait* we are told that Stephen Dedalus had this right
at Belvedere (84), and also that he was "firm in habits of quiet
obedience" (93, 181). He seems, in fact, to have been a model
student (183). But even then, when he was most intensely religious, he found it difficult to enter into the Jesuit spirit: "to
merge his life in the common tide of other lives was harder for
him than any fasting or prayer" (175), and he soon realized that
he could never be part of any movement or devote himself whole-
heartedly to any popular cause: "His destiny was to be elusive of
social or religious orders" (188). But this was merely negative.

For rebellion against the Jesuit life of obedience he had yet to have some intimation of a positive course he could follow as an individual. When it came, he rebelled; for he saw then that intellectual meekness would be fatal to his integrity as an artist, and that if he was to do his own work he must be his own man. In this respect at least, Stephen's life paralleled that of Joyce; and with whatever detachment the author viewed his hero, there is reason to believe that on religion and on art their views were identical.

In *Dubliners,* accordingly, obedience is presented as weakness or vice. Farrington of "Counterparts" obeys his employer to the point of degradation; Kathleen Kearney of "A Mother" silently swallows her humiliation and acquiesces in Mrs. Kearney's vulgar display of acquisitiveness, though it is in her power to take matters into her own hands. But perhaps the most insidious form of intellectual obedience is that which we yield not to any particular authority but to what John Jay Chapman called the atmospheric pressure; it is a matter of being sensible and accommodating oneself to the facts or the circumstances. This also the Jesuits practice,[11] and this also Joyce would not practice; he presents it as the vice of several people in *Dubliners.* Jimmy Doyle of "After the Race" spends an afternoon and a night in activities he doesn't really enjoy, dutifully drinks himself into a stupor and remorsefully gambles away more than he can afford, in the company of people he hardly knows, because these are the conventions of what he calls "seeing life" (56), and it never occurs to him that he doesn't have to see life. Bob Doran of "The Boarding House" is an atheist by conviction who goes to church, a celibate by instinct who has an affair with a vulgar girl, and a bachelor by choice who marries, impelled in each case by "all the weight of social opinion" (78). The distraught young girl of "Eveline" is crushed by the same weight. Little Chandler of "A Little Cloud" is "a prisoner for life" (104) to what he calls his "unfortunate timidity" (99), an extreme sensitivity to public opinion. He dreams of being a poet, not an original poet but one whom "the English critics, perhaps, would recognise . . . as one of the Celtic school by reason of the melancholy tone of his poems; besides that, he would put in allusions" (90). It doesn't occur to him that this sort of thing is no "higher" than Gallaher's "tawdry journalism" (99), since it involves conforming to the preconceptions of a tame audience rather than writing to his own requirements—in fact, he has no requirements of his own; nor does it occur to him that Gallaher too is a prisoner for life— a prisoner of the most abject kind, who lives in the prison by choice and doesn't realize where he is.

But it is in "Grace" that Joyce's scorn of the Jesuits' accommodation to the facts is made explicit and unmistakable. Here a group of businessmen, seeking to rescue a friend from incipient alcoholism, induce him to attend a retreat, where they will all confess their sins and "wash the pot together" (207). They assure their friend that there will be nothing strenuous or difficult about it—"O, it's just a retreat" (209)—that the Jesuit Father Purdon won't be too hard on them because he is a man of the world like themselves (209), that his sermon will be "just a kind of a friendly talk, you know, in a common-sense way" (210), and that all they have to do is to stand up with lighted candles in their hands and repeat their baptismal vows (218). If this seems too slack, easy, uninspired and uninspiring to have any value, let us remember that in religion Jesuitism is the science of the possible. "That low man seeks a little thing to do,/ Sees it and does it," and the Society of Jesus helps him. Saint Ignatius opens his *Spiritual Exercises* with instructions for confessors and for directors of retreats:

> The Spiritual Exercises ought to be suited to the disposition of those who wish to make them, that is to say, according to their age, learning, or talent, lest to one untutored or of weak constitution be given things which he cannot bear without inconvenience, and by which he cannot profit. . . . If he who gives the Exercises perceives that the exercitant is of limited understanding and naturally of little capacity, so that from him much fruit is not expected, it will be fitting to give him some of the easier Exercises, until he confess his sins, and then giving him some examination of conscience, and a method of more frequent confession, than

was his custom, so that he may preserve what he has gained, it will be better not to proceed further.[12]

Father Purdon accordingly adapts his discourse to his audience:

> He told his hearers that he was there that evening for no terrifying, no extravagant purpose; but as a man of the world speaking to his fellowmen. He came to speak to businessmen and he would speak to them in a businesslike way. If he might use the metaphor, he said, he was their spiritual accountant; and he wished each and every one of his hearers to open his books, the books of his spiritual life, and see if they tallied with conscience (222).

The whole burden of his friendly talk is that Jesus Christ is not a hard taskmaster but only wants them to correct any errors there may be in their accounts. This is straight out of the *Spiritual Exercises*. The exercitant is instructed to examine his soul twice daily, at midday and after supper, for particular sins and for the general tenor of his thoughts, words and deeds. At the first Particular Examen he is to concentrate on a

> particular sin or defect, . . . demanding an account from his soul concerning the particular fault in question which he desires to correct and amend, reviewing the time elapsed hour by hour, or period by period, from the hour at which he rose till the hour and moment of the present examination, and let him mark on the first line of the figure D‑‑‑‑‑‑ as many points as there are times he has fallen into that particular sin or defect; and then let him resolve anew to amend himself during the interval between this and the second examination.[13]

After supper he is to repeat the process:

> As the first line of the figure D‑‑‑‑‑ represents the first examination, and the second the second, let him at night see

whether from the first line to the second . . . any improve-
ment has taken place.[14]

The exercitant is urged to keep such accounts from day to day
and from week to week, so that he can plainly see his progress or
lack of progress. Similarly, the chief point of the general exam-
ination is "to demand an account of my soul, first of my thoughts,
then of my words, lastly of my actions, in the same way as has
been explained in the Particular Examen." [15] All in all, this involves quite a bit of bookkeeping. Doubtless it is an effective
method of overcoming bad habits, provided they are not symp-
toms of radical deficiencies or contradictions in the exercitant's
life; it is essentially the same method as that of having children
keep charts to show that they have brushed their teeth and
washed their hands; its effectiveness for stopping the incipient
alcoholism of an unsuccessful businessman may be questioned;
in any case the distaste of such an individualist as Joyce is understandable. For the irony with which in maturity he recorded
a commercial metaphor of Stephen's adolescence in the *Portrait*
—"he seemed to feel his soul in devotion pressing like fingers the
keyboard of a great cash register and to see the amount of his
purchase start forth immediately in heaven" (171)—not only
refers to the stated value of prayers in terms of years of purgatory
remitted, but also has its straight-faced counterpart in a letter
of Saint Ignatius to a woman who had lost her sister: "I am
certain on many grounds and from many signs that in the other
life she is full of glory without end, where I trust, so long as we
do not forget her in our prayers however unworthy and poor, she
in her turn will favour and repay us with holy interest." [16]
This mechanization and quantitative standardization of the
motions of the spirit would alone have been enough to alienate
Joyce; but closely related to it was the even more alien practice
of deliberately abasing the individual, whose affections, good or
bad, were liable to be "inordinate" unless directed by devout intention to the glory of God. The confessing sinner is exhorted
to see himself as "an ulcer and abscess whence have issued so
many sins and so many iniquities, and such vile poison." [17]
When Stephen confessed in the *Portrait,* "His sins . . . trickled

in shameful drops from his soul festering and oozing like a sore"
(166). This attitude is of course not confined to the Jesuits. That
disgust with the body which exhales from so much of medieval
poetry [18] is part of the general denigration of personality that informs the thought of the Middle Ages and later of the Counter-
Renaissance, and which is still with us in such writers as T. S.
Eliot, Aldous Huxley, Evelyn Waugh and José Ortega y Gasset.
In Saint Anselm's *Cur Deus Homo,* God is an irascible Norman
baron and the human race a pack of filthy insubordinate Saxon
churls. The belief that there is a fundamental antagonism between man and God, that the honor of one requires the complete
submission of the other, seems to be implicit in the notion of
an all-powerful God—that is, in monotheism. In the Western
world it goes back at least as far as Plato. Though seldom expressed with such naïve enthusiasm as Anselm's, it has always
been a very useful conception for keeping the *id* under control
and for maintaining the authority of the temporal barons. In
fact, the only way the church could keep man's soul from complete damnation was to split God into three parts, the first to
damn, the second to save, and the third to reconcile the other
two; but in order to avoid a polytheistic division of authority it
had to insist that the three were identical in will and in power.
This is so hard to grasp that Saint Anselm admits (in the *Monologium*) that it cannot be explained or even understood.[19] He
falls back on faith, as do all pious logicians from Boethius to
Ockham, confessing that their science is of no avail for apprehension of the inexplicable splendor. But it remained for Saint
Ignatius to reduce to a code of rules their pious abandon and
the concomitant abasement of the individual personality; if at
times it seems to us that he threw out the bath merely as a pre-
text for getting rid of the baby, let us remember that, whatever
his successors may have been, Ignatius himself was a sincere man
insofar as sincerity is possible to creatures who understand themselves as imperfectly as we do. A stupid man cannot be sincere;
with Ignatius, as with everyone else, the question of sincerity is
partly a question of intelligence, and we know that in that respect he was not deficient. He really believed that the will of the
church was the will of God, and the individual a small, weak,

ignorant and depraved insignificance, who has no value except as he may be used for God's purposes. Thus, the fourth point of the second Spiritual Exercise is "to consider who God is, against whom I have sinned, looking at His attributes, comparing them with their contraries in myself: His wisdom with my ignorance, His omnipotence with my weakness, His justice with my iniquity, His goodness with my malice [i.e., *malitia,* wickedness]." [20]

The Exercises accordingly conclude with a set of "Rules for Thinking with the Church," in which we are exhorted to lay aside "all private judgment" and "obey in all things . . . the Hierarchical Church." We are not only to obey but to praise the church and everything connected with it, from the sacraments to "the buildings and the ornaments" and "the constitutions, recommendations, and habits of life of our superiors." If these are not "praiseworthy," we must not say so "in public discourse, or before the lower classes," though "it may be useful to speak of their bad habits to those who can apply a remedy." The proper intellectual attitude is summed up in Paragraph 365: "To attain the truth in all things, we ought always to hold that we believe what seems to us white to be black, if the Hierarchical Church so defines it"; and the whole is concluded with an exhortation to serve God not only out of love but also out of fear:

> . . . because not only is filial fear a pious and most holy thing, but even servile fear, when a man does not rise to anything better and more useful, is of great help to him to escape from mortal sin; and, after he has escaped from it, he easily attains to filial fear, which is altogether acceptable and pleasing to God our Lord, because it is inseparable from Divine love.[21]

For people of democratic impulses this fearlove is hard to understand; perhaps it is what the citizens of Oceania feel for Big Brother; perhaps it is what Ortega y Gasset thinks commoners should feel for the aristocracy, or white-trash Southerners think Negroes should feel for them; perhaps it is the quality lacking which a son may neglect to touch his cap to his father—an offense for which, Aldous Huxley tells us in "Comfort," Vespasiano

Gonzaga kicked his only son to death, thereby upholding what Huxley calls decorum and good manners. This in any case is what it meant to Joyce. In *Finnegans Wake,* Shaun as teacher instructs all the world: "Gentes and laitymen, fullstoppers and semicolonials, hybreds and lubberds!" He informs this varied audience that since they are all indiscriminately "muddlecrass pupils, . . . a squad of urchins, snifflynosed, goslingnecked, clothyheaded, tangled in your lacings, tingled in your pants, etsiteraw etcicero," he will put his moral lesson in the form of a parable, the fable of the Mookse and the Gripes. He identifies himself with the Mookse, who is not only God, onesome, impermeable, impugnable, immobile and immortal (152), but also Popes Adrian, Leo (153), Clement, Urban, Eugenius, Celestius, Gregory (154) and Pius (156), the Fourth, the Fifth, the Sixth, the Seventh, the Forty-Fifth and the Forty-Ninth (153). Incensed at the Gripes' presuming to greet him, he bellows, "Hang you for an animal rurale! I am superbly in my supremest poncif! Abase you, baldyqueens! Gather behind me, satraps! . . . Let you be Beeton. And let me be Los Angeles. Now measure your length. Now estimate my capacity. Well, sour?" (154).[22] The third point of the Meditation on Sins, says Ignatius,

> is to consider who I am, abasing myself by examples; first how little I am in comparison with all men; secondly, what men are in comparison with all the angels and saints of Paradise; thirdly, to consider what all that is created is in comparison with God; then I alone, what can I be?

The meditation is to be concluded with "a colloquy of mercy, reasoning and giving thanks to God our Lord, for having given me life till now, and proposing through His grace to amend henceforward." [23] But the self-respecting Gripes cannot submit; like Socrates, he prefers to die rather than live on the Mookse's terms. To the Mookse's assertion that after a thousand years of starvation he will be "belined [blind, adjusted] to the world," he replies that after a thousand years the Mookse's goat will be still more bothered. The term is ambiguous, since he himself is the Mookse's sacrificial goat; but one of its meanings is faintly reminiscent of Socrates' defiance on being sentenced to death and of Giordano Bruno's statement, "Perhaps you who pronounce my sentence are in greater fear than I who receive it." [24]

This theme is repeated throughout *Finnegans Wake:* the power, arrogance and corporate assurance of those who presume to speak for God, opposed by the intelligence, skepticism and lonely self-respect of the creative individual. There are weaknesses on both sides: on the individual's, the importunity of the flesh and the hesitancy that comes of understanding the complexity of his relationship with the others; on the side of those who presumably speak for God, the blindness of action uninhibited by doubt, thought, understanding or compassion. It has always been thus, says Joyce; at the beginning of the world, when the Allhighest first spoke, "his nuptial eagles sharped their beaks of prey" (80).

This is a terrible indictment; it amounts to a denial of God in the name of the human individual, who cannot live with Him; it is, in fact, the obverse of the Jesuit denial of the individual self in the name of God. The Mookse and the Gripes, symbols respectively of authority and independence, are always in the background of *Finnegans Wake,* both before and after their brief appearance as the central characters of an episode. Earwicker is denounced in "mooxed metaphores" (70); his drunken roomer, who has much in common with Shem, before leaving the house pegs a few smooth stones at the wicked wicket "by way of final mocks for his gropes" (72). Shaun as professor, who has more in common with Shem than he will permit himself to know, inadvertently admits that Shem appeals to his "gropesarching eyes" (176). Shem's internal conflicts are diagnosed: "Mookery mooks, it's a grippe of his gripes" (231). Because of his quixotism he is "most gripously . . . bedizzled and debuzzled," but his brother, "Sin Showpanza, . . . the kerl he left behind him," stands among "the green heroes . . . mookst kevinly" (234). The book the twins study in the Triv and Quad episode says, "You're holy mooxed and gaping up the wrong palce" (299). A customer in Earwicker's tavern predicts the coming of the "allbleakest age . . . what with his Marx and their Groups" (365).

The Gracehoper admits to the Ondt that the Leapyear Girls will probably never "quit your mocks for my gropes" (418). In Jaun's sententious speech he concedes, "There's no plagues like rome. It gives up the gripes" (465). Under interrogation, Yawn professes a fondness for his brother: "Fullgrapce for an endupper, half muxy on his whole" (489). One of the mottoes on Earwicker's walls is "Mind the Monks and their Grasps" (579). Referring to the Crimean War, ALP says, "Olobobo, ye foxy theagues! The moskors thought to ball you out" (622).

Thus, throughout the book, authority implies unquestioning obedience, and independence a compulsive disobedience that belies its own nature. That is why independence is always defeated but never gives up the struggle. In the Triv and Quad episode the good Kev's marginal comments are of three kinds: expressions of assent such as "sic" (260); harmless but revealing signposts such as "incipit intermissio" (278) and "sortes virginianae" [*sic*] (281); and clumsy efforts to explain the text by means of formulas which he quotes without understanding. These formulas are: scholastic—"constitution of the constitutionable as constitutional" (261) and "gnosis of procreate determination" (262); romantic German philosophical—"probapossible prolegomena to ideareal history" (262); Viconian and modern anthropological-historical—"the localisation of legend leading to the legalisation of latifundism" (264) and "early notions of acquired rights and the influence of collective tradition upon the individual" (268). In all his comments there is no dissent or even any question. He accepts the text as given, even when he doesn't understand it. But skepticism, independence and irreverence mark all the bad Dolph's comments. At the first mention of God he writes in the margin, "With his broad and hairy face, to Ireland a disgrace" (260). To the cabalistic name of God, "Ainsoph," he puts a footnote, "Groupname for grapejuice" (261), implying that God is a product of the vine and also that He inheres generically in the Gripes, of all people. To the book's pious "At maturing daily gloryaims" (a gray-flannel-suitish version of *Ad majorem Dei gloriam,* the motto of the Society of Jesus), he puts the footnote, "Lawdy Dawdy simpers"—*Laude Daude semper,* Praise-Schmaise forever (282).[25] On Saint Augustine's "O felicitous culpability!" he comments, "Hearsay in paradox lust" (263) [26]—accusing Augustine of falling into heresy through his rhetorician's lust for paradoxes—and apropos of nothing, "Bet ye fippence anythesious there's no puggatory, are yous game?" (266). For his irreverence Kev blacks his eye and knocks him out (304); they are seemingly reconciled (304–305) and "singulfied" (306), finish their lessons peaceably, and send a joint Christmas greeting to their parents; but at the very end Dolph thumbs his nose (an act which he says is the sign of the Antichrist), and for the traditional *chi*, initial of Christ or Christmas, symbol of a kiss and "crisscross" or Christ's cross (11, 111, 624), draws two crossed bones badly gnawed (308), traditional sign of death. The encounters of the Ondt and the Gracehoper, Justius and Mercius, Burrus and Caseous, and Chuff and Glugg end similarly, with victory for the obedient brother, seeming reconciliation, and final defiance by the disobedient brother. Though defeated, he is not reconciled; he does not yield up his hate either for a caress or for a blow.[27] Thus he gains a moral or Platonic victory, a victory of essence over ape, of principle over circumstance. In Joyce's world it is the church which is cold, pragmatic and opportunistic; the creative, anti-ecclesiastical individual who lives by principle; and though in the struggle between them the church wins outwardly, the individual becomes godlike by asserting the best that is in him, by saying against all odds, "I am." This is the fulfillment of Stephen's vision in the *Portrait:* the free, fully integrated human personality, which by virtue of its wholeness, harmony and radiance is in a sense imperishable (196–197, 299): the artist who can mirror perfectly "an inner world of individual emotions" (194) or the man who, though he is not an artist, succeeds in expressing his unique nature through his "mode of life" (291).

For the artist, however—as we shall see—the fulfillment is both more complex and less nearly complete than for the practical man. He cannot rest in disobedience; his rewards are of a different kind. But before we consider the artist's difficulties, let us see how the practical man goes about achieving freedom.

In *Finnegans Wake* the vision is fulfilled by mythical figures and abstract archetypes; in *Ulysses* it is fulfilled by an advertising salesman presented with the most minute concreteness. This is not to say that it can be fulfilled by everyone—for Bloom is no ordinary man. He is an enchanted prince, an Apollo under penance bound to serve the most ordinary of men, a lost angel like Proust's Françoise, one of those "creatures who . . . , doomed by a harsh fate to live among the simple-minded, . . . were, so to speak, all members, though scattered, straying, robbed of their heritage of reason, of the celestial family." [28] He is—and this is Joyce's great paradox—a Platonic or Christian soul, imprisoned in gross flesh and so exiled from God who is its home. Bloom could have said with Ignatius, no ordinary man either, "My soul is imprisoned in this corruptible body, and my whole self in this vale of misery, as it were in exile among brute beasts." [29] Where Joyce differs from the church, and most emphatically from Ignatius, is in asserting that not only the Kingdom of God but Godhead itself is within us. This is one possible interpretation; another is that Bloom—unlike, say, Boylan or Menton—has God's grace. A good case could be made for the second interpretation; but, as so often in Joyce, neither interpretation excludes the other. In either case, our task is to assert the divinity in us or to manifest the grace of God; and this is so difficult that it is beyond the strength of most of us, for it involves defiance of all worldly powers, including—in Joyce's view —the church. This feat our salesman accomplishes.

Every great novel is the story of a miracle. The miracle of *Ulysses* is not Bloom's journey through "the rubbish-world . . . saturated with death and *Kitsch*," [30] through parts of which every man journeys every day, but his rising above it. He rises by defiance, by disobedience, by standing apart from and against all its values. For him this is especially difficult, since the leading motive of his life up to the day we see him has been to be accepted by the world. For one who, like Bloom, is inherently different from worldly men, the search for acceptance is as delusive as the conscious search for happiness; it has in fact led him not to acceptance but to rejection. Since he is not a creative person, he does need to be accepted; but only when he accepts himself, asserts his very real superiority, defies his rejectors and stands on his own terms does such a markedly different man become acceptable. The world accepts him because it has no choice.

Bloom's day begins inauspiciously, with obedience and deference to his insolent cat (55) and his contemptuous wife (56, 61ff.). Nevertheless, the ultimate assertion of his own will is latent in much of his conduct throughout the day—in his fine perception of the cattiness of the cat (55–56), his dismissal of the "kind of stuff you read" about the Middle East (57), his hard-headed reflections at Dignam's funeral (106–114), his kind but clear observation of the blind stripling (178–180), his detachment in the Ormond bar (252–286), etc. But all his moments of detachment, difference, self-assertion, freedom, are interspersed with other moments of self-denial, self-abasement, false adaptability and open defeat. Not until he is brutally attacked by The Citizen does he consciously make a stand—and even then with reservations (336). In his defiance he does not altogether renounce the world. With the essential, necessary, saving inconsistency of the liberal humanist, he takes his stand with the great Jewish deniers of the world, Marx, Spinoza and Christ, and also with certain Jews who successfully adapted themselves to it, Mendelssohn and Mercadante. Even in this, as it happens, he is deluded, for with one exception the men he mentions were not nominally Jews: Marx, Mendelssohn and Mercadante were baptized Christians, the first was anti-Semitic, the latter two wrote church music, and Spinoza was excommunicated from the Jewish faith. The only one of Bloom's heroes who remained a Jew to the end was Jesus, who on the last night of his life celebrated the Passover. (Joyce is always rich in irony!) Nevertheless, Bloom's will and intention are right; in one sentence he undoes all the baptisms and all the denials on both sides, restoring to all Jewish individuals their Jewishness, their individuality, their dignity. This is the beginning of his own catharsis and redemption. He undergoes metempsychosis: he becomes Elijah, transfigured, godlike (339).

In the Nausicaä episode he slips back badly into the rubbish (359–360), and in the Circe episode it overwhelms and all but annihilates him (518ff.). Each of these experiences is necessary, for in each he faces the facts and admits the truth about himself,

a process without which salvation is impossible. Gerty Mac-
Dowell is no confessor and Bella Cohen is no psychoanalyst; but
Gerty witnesses and forgives his sin, though she does not understand it (361), and Bella, though she does not forgive him, makes
him understand himself and so gain control over his behavior.
Having passed through the deep Hell of self-knowledge, he opens
the window for air (566) and takes command of the situation
(568). Leaving Bella Cohen's establishment in order to save
Dedalus, he is temporarily disconcerted by "the hue and cry"
of his own guilty conscience, the sense of his own unworthiness
to undertake anything decent (570–571), but when he sees the
actual crowd around Dedalus he banishes these phantoms, asserts himself, and begins to be accepted by others (588ff.).

How far this acceptance will go and how long it will last we
don't know. The experiences of the afternoon and evening make
possible the reassertion of his position as master in his own home
and Molly's startled acceptance of it "because he never did a
thing like that before" (723); but whether she will accept it in
the morning is a question. On the evidence of her soliloquy, the
best that can be said is that she is of two minds. She resists the
notion of getting his breakfast (749, 763), but plans to do it (758,
765); she resists the notion of resuming sexual relations with him
(729), but entertains it (727, 732, 762); in her thoughts he blends
with Boylan (727, 738–739) and Stephen (760, 765). Boylan has
promised to return on Monday (732), and she can hardly wait
(739); and for Stephen's sake she dreams of improving her mind
(761) and her appearance (765); she recognizes, however, that
Bloom is a gentleman (727, 732, 767), and wishes to arouse his
old desire for her (766). She has been and is still jealous of every
woman he looks at, whether a servant (724–725), a friend (728),
or a shopgirl (737–738). She is sure Bloom has deliberately
thrown Boylan in her way (751) in order to deprive her of a
superior moral position with regard to his own philandering
(725), but she assures herself that at least he isn't in love with
anyone else (723). Moreover, the possible physical consequences
of her afternoon with Boylan are washed away in the menstrual
flood (754); since it is now Friday morning, she may very well
not be able to have sexual relations with Boylan on Monday, and

during the rest of the week she and Bloom are to be deprived of
Boylan's services (732–733); however, she does not think the
novelty of a hotel bed will excite Bloom to anything more than
"fooling," and regrets only that she can hardly tell him not to
bother her (732). As for the future of their relationship, there
seems to be about as much and as little warrant for Edmund
Wilson's cheerful conclusion [31] as for Harry Levin's sad one.[32]

But the question need not be settled, because it is really irrelevant. Molly is not Gea-Tellus (721) but rather a swine, and
for a person of any sensitivity no life with her could be good. In
their past relationship only the swine in Bloom was engaged,
and there is no reason to believe that she could engage the other
elements of his character in the future. But this too is irrelevant,
for Bloom himself has finally reasserted the other elements. This
is what matters. Like Plato's good man, he is henceforth in-
vulnerable by outward circumstances, for he knows that he is
what he is. Whether he succeeds or fails in business, in love, in
social life, is of no importance; for his goodness, mixed and
blended as it is with evil, is indestructible. His assertion of it
may have no effect on others, but it has had an effect on himself:
he has been reborn: he *is*. Through disobedience he has achieved
being, moral being; and he will continue to disobey, regardless of
consequences.

For Stephen, however, the achievement of moral being is a
more complex and difficult matter; for though as a person he
must refuse obedience to those who would exact it, as an artist
he must recognize that obedience, subordination and hierarchy
are values that many people live by. Though we reject the Grand
Inquisitor's view, the moral impact and artistic truth of his appearance in *The Brothers Karamazov* are absolutely dependent
on our recognition that there is something in what he says. If he
were talking patent nonsense there would be no dramatic tension
and no artistic value in his disputing God; as it is, though we
may be morally or socially or politically offended by what he
says, we are not artistically offended. Every artist's life is haunted
by the truth he must work by, a truth pithily stated by Friedrich
Hebbel, that in the drama "all characters must be in the right."
This truth implies another: that all characters must be in the

wrong. This second truth is perhaps more strictly true than the first, for if Hamlet or Oedipus were merely in the right we could have no fellow feeling for either, whereas if they were merely in the wrong we might—as we do, say, for Camus' Meursault. If Stephen Dedalus were merely in the right he would be insufferable; we applaud his strength only because we share his weakness; we are eager for him to win because it is far from certain that he can.

This is true of our feeling for Bloom also; the difference is that Stephen, being more fully aware of the complex interplay of values in life, cannot limit himself to the role of defiant hero. To his mind it would be as constricting, as incomplete and false, as the role of conformist. I suspect that a sudden appreciation of this point was the real reason for Joyce's throwing the manuscript of *Stephen Hero* into the fire. In the *Portrait* Stephen is less aggressive, less completely right, less consistently victorious, and therefore more sympathetic; in *Ulysses* the elements of weakness in his character are further emphasized, and in *Finnegans Wake* Shem is never seen except through the hostile eyes of Shaun, his bad points being elaborated in full detail and his good ones revealed only by inadvertence.

Likewise, in *Stephen Hero* Stephen argues with everybody and always wins; in the *Portrait* the argument often ends inconclusively or stupidly and Stephen is frustrated; in *Ulysses* he generally avoids argument, and in *Finnegans Wake,* as Shem, the artist always loses the argument. The situation being thus reversed, the nature of the artist's reward is changed. It has become internalized. He is like Paul Valéry's great man, whose errors and defeats don't count. "Even his ruin exalts him." Not that his enemies understand anything of all that. What arouses Shaun's most nearly sincere contempt is Shem's un-Jesuitical willingness to allow some truth to every point of view:

> He went without saying that the cull disliked anything anyway approaching a plain straightforward standup or knockdown row and, as often as he was called in to umpire any octagonal argument among slangwhangers, the accomplished washout always used to rub shoulders with the last speaker

and clasp shakers (the handtouch which is speech without
words) and agree to every word as soon as half uttered, command me!, your servant, good, I revere you, how, my seer?
be drinking that! quite truth, gratias, I'm yoush, see wha'm
hearing?, also goods, please it, me sure?, be filling this!,
quiso, you said it, apasafello, muchas grassyass, is there
firing-on-me?, is their girlic-on-you?, to your good self, your
sulphur, and then at once focuss his whole unbalanced attention upon the next octagonist who managed to catch a
listener's eye, asking and imploring him out of his piteous
onewinker, (*hemoptysia diadumenos*) whether there was anything in the world he could do to please him and to overflow
his tumbletantaliser for him yet once more (174).

But there is of course more in Shem's attitude than the shifty
agreeableness of a barfly. What Shaun will never understand is
that an artist must be a relativist as surely as a moralist must not;
and the difficulty is compounded by the fact that no man is
merely an artist or merely a moralist, but every man who is
genuinely one is also to some extent the other. "There's a touch
of the artist about old Bloom," says Lenehan in *Ulysses* (232),
and surely there is more than a touch of the moralist about
young Stephen. This fact, I believe, accounts for the fascination
of each by the other. They are mutually attracted, but they can
never make satisfactory contact. They communicate across an
enormous distance, vaguely. Stephen's clearer awareness of the
difficulty makes him decline the closer relationship that Bloom
suggests, but it would be impossible in any case. Bloom's future
course is one of simple stubborn disobedience; Stephen consciously chooses to disobey, but realizes at the same time that the
values he denies have an evident claim on many fairly decent
people.

Thus Joyce's final attitude toward the Jesuits is (pardon me)
ambivalent; for though if he is to function as an artist he must
struggle free of their moral grip, he must also as an artist take
them into account, not merely as straw men to be knocked down,
as in *Stephen Hero,* but as representatives of an attitude that
does a great deal to make human life what it is. Not that he

approves of life as it is; he merely recognizes it as a fact. His morality is therefore as different from Bloom's as from Mulligan's; his conscience is neither that of a conformist nor altogether that of a rebel, but the permanently uneasy conscience of an artist.

CHAPTER VII

Art and Fortitude: Applied Aquinas

"Art, being concerned with making, is not concerned with doing."—Aristotle, *Nicomachean Ethics*, VI, 3.

THERE ARE THREE KINDS OF LOST LEADERS: THOSE WHO STOP FIGHTing, those who go over to the enemy, and those whom the enemy appropriates after their deaths; but these last are not wholly lost. Aquinas' theology, like Aristotle's philosophy, was first condemned as heretical and later prescribed as the standard of orthodoxy; thus, in each case, an independent thinker was domesticated and made a means of discouraging independent thought. But the provocative virtue of ideas is never dead, and there is always a danger that when it strikes an active mind the results may be different from what orthodoxy requires. To the extent that education is a matter of inculcating ideas, in the literal sense of stamping them in, it must fail with the most thoughtful students. "Perhaps Aquinas would understand me better than you," Stephen tells the docile Lynch in the *Portrait*. "He was a poet himself" (246). A poet: a maker: a creative individual. There was no incongruity in Joyce's deriving from such a source the foundation of his aesthetic theory and a reasoned justification of his lonely fortitude.

For Aquinas was a poet not only in his hymns but in his treatises. Certainly the *Summa Theologica,* though built in air like the pleasure dome of the delighted Coleridge, is a masterpiece of intellectual craftsmanship that affords an essentially

Notes to Chapter VII begin on page 158.

aesthetic pleasure to those who care for work well done; this pleasure Aquinas knew himself, and it underlies all his statements about art. Though, as Stephen says in the *Portrait,* these tell him nothing about "the phenomena of artistic conception, artistic gestation and artistic reproduction" (for reasons we shall see), he adds that so far as the work of art itself and the beholder's pleasure in it are concerned, Aquinas will carry him "all along the line" (245–246).

In *Ulysses,* in an altogether different connection, Stephen says he enjoys reading Aquinas' fat volumes in the original (203). Since at this point he has long since renounced Catholicism, particularly the Thomistic Catholicism of the Jesuits, it is evident that his enjoyment is literary and aesthetic. The two artists would doubtless understand each other, for this reason and also because their views of art, within the limits noted, are identical. Stephen's conception of the work of art as having "wholeness, harmony and radiance" is quoted directly from the *Summa Theologica* (I, Q. 39, Art. 8) [1] and is so fully explained in the *Portrait* (248ff.) that it needs no further comment; but since Joyce does not mention the passages of the *Summa* that confirm and in part account for his view of the artist's independence of non-artistic values, and since also they anticipate the aesthetics of Joyce's master Flaubert, it may be worth while to point them out.

Anything made by art or skill, says Aquinas, is external to the artist; it has its own independent existence and its own virtue. This of course is derived from Aristotle's *Nicomachean Ethics,* II, 4, which states further that the ethical quality of an act depends on the intention as well as on the result but that the quality of a thing made inheres entirely in the thing itself. Having thus briefly distinguished between the arts and the virtues, Aristotle passes on to other points; Aquinas takes up this one and develops its implications. The only relevant question to ask about a work of art as such, he says, is how well it is made. Questions about its possible good or evil uses and social effects are irrelevant; so are questions about the good or evil intent of the artist in making it, and so are questions about the artist's personal character and private life:

The good of an art is to be found, not in the craftsman, but in the product of the art . . . : for since the making of a thing passes into external matter, [art] is a perfection not of the maker, but of the thing made. . . . Consequently art does not require of the craftsman that his act be a good act, but that his work be good . . . (e.g., that a knife should carve well, or that a saw should cut well). . . . Wherefore the craftsman needs art, not that he may live well, but that he may produce a good work of art (II. I, Q. 57, Art. 5, Reply Obj. 1).[2]

Art is thus completely amoral. For upright living, which Aquinas, following Aristotle, calls "prudence," we need of course

a moral virtue, which rectifies the appetite. On the other hand, the good of things made by art is not the good of man's appetite, but the good of the things themselves: wherefore art does not presuppose rectitude of the appetite. The consequence is that more praise is given to a craftsman who is at fault willingly, than to one who is unwillingly; whereas it is more contrary to prudence to sin willingly than unwillingly, since rectitude of the will is essential to prudence, but not to art (II. I, Q. 7, Art. 4. Cf. II. I, Q. 57, Art. 3; Q. 58, Arts. 4–5; Aristotle, *Nichomachean Ethics*, VI, 5).

Oscar Wilde hardly went farther; at this point we should be only slightly surprised to read that an ethical sympathy in an artist is an unpardonable mannerism of style. T. S. Eliot told Virginia Woolf that Joyce was strongly influenced by Pater and Newman;[3] certainly the prose of the *Portrait* shows these influences (though it is not true that Joyce was "a purely literary writer"); Stephen enjoyed Newman's "cloistral silverveined prose" (*Portrait,* 204), and doubtless Pater's ideas of art were congenial to the young man who wanted his epiphanies printed on green oval leaves (*Ulysses,* 41); but Joyce himself, in the *Portrait,* called his own aesthetics "applied Aquinas" (245), and we shall see that this was literally true. Neither Pater's aesthetics

nor Newman's could have led to *Dubliners;* Aquinas' could and
did.

So far, Aquinas has used the word "art" in the Greek sense of
skill, craft, or craftsmanship; but what he says is applicable to art
in the aesthetic sense, with which he is also concerned and on
which his views are surprisingly modern. Since a work of art is
good in proportion to the skill with which it is made, its subject
matter is irrelevant to any consideration of its quality; he sup-
ports this conclusion, on its subjective side, by the authority of
Aristotle:

> Representations of things, even of those which are not
> pleasant in themselves, give rise to pleasure; for the soul
> rejoices in comparing one thing with another, because com-
> parison of one thing with another is the proper and con-
> natural act of reason, as the Philosopher says (*Poetics,* IV)
> (II. I, Q. 32, Art. 8).

This would certainly apply to such passages in *Ulysses* as the
descriptions of Paddy Dignam's funeral (99–114), of the Burton
restaurant (166–168) and of Nighttown (422–423). Here our disgust with the subject matter is overcome by our admiration of
apt and perfect language, so that we are raised above disgust.
The enjoyment of art is thus an intellectual pleasure.[4] As such,
its nature is passive, since both understanding and pleasure are
passive states. The divine intellect, in which all being pre-exists
and from which all being is actualized, is pure activity—play;
but the human intellect, finite and far removed from such perfection,

> is at first *like a clean tablet on which nothing is written,* as
> the Philosopher says (*De Anima,* III, 4). This is made clear
> by the fact, that at first we are only in potentiality to under-
> stand, and afterwards we are made to understand. . . . And
> consequently the intellect is a passive power. . . . The
> operation of the apprehensive power is likened to rest (I, Q.
> 79, Art. 2; Q. 81, Art. 1).[5]

However, since particular things are not intelligible as such (I, Q. 86, Art. 1; cf. Aristotle, *Posterior Analytics,* I, 31), there is need for an active intellect to make them intelligible by abstracting their genera and species (I, Q. 79, Art. 3). The active intellect exists, but is separate from the soul; it is not a part of man, but is "God Himself," from whom "the human soul derives its intellectual light" (I, Q. 79, Art. 4). This is why Aquinas has nothing to say about the problems of artistic conception, gestation and reproduction: for him, the active intellect in man has no function but to abstract, and the passive intellect none but to contemplate. The human mind can thus understand and enjoy, within limits, but cannot create: "God alone can create" (I, Q. 90, Art. 3). Thus, for Aquinas, art is not a creative process; it is altogether a matter of imitation, with whatever of artifice or technical skill this may involve. Stephen therefore, in the *Portrait,* needs "a new terminology and a new personal experience" for the side of his aesthetic that deals with creation (246).

But if Aquinas has nothing to say to the creative personality, he has some very cogent things to say to the spectator or consumer of art, about the nature of beauty and of the pleasure we take in it; thus the artist, since he is also a particularly sensitive consumer, can find in Aquinas a partial basis for his work. Of course this last statement is true only if the artist accepts Aquinas' view; but Joyce was by temperament inclined to such a view, both because it recognizes the moral indifference of the dedicated artist and the resulting conflict between the artist and the social man (even though both be in the same person) and because it recognizes as the end of art an arrest or stasis of the soul.

This latter was for Joyce an ideal condition, to which his own soul rarely attained. In the *Portrait* he tells us twice that Stephen is incapable of strong or sustained emotion (91–92, 172–173), but these passages are radically inconsistent with others in which he describes Stephen as "proud and sensitive and suspicious, battling against the squalor of his life and against the riot of his mind," given to "futile enthusiasms" and "mad and filthy orgies" (102)— a person who blushes with pride (183) and speaks on political matters with "scorn and anger" (227) or "cold violence" (238).

His heart is "easily embittered" (222); his soul is filled by turns with "ecstasy" and with "rude, brutal anger" (258). Sylvia Beach recalls Joyce's "extreme sensibility," which made him blush "over trifles"; [6] so far was he from being imperturbable, in fact, that in *Finnegans Wake* he hit back at the "damned cheek" of the poor hack who had reviewed *Ulysses* in that "Anglican ordinal" the *Sporting Times*—"The Pink 'Un" (185). Stuart Gilbert's statement that every word Joyce wrote was chosen for aesthetic rather than personal reasons is an exaggeration.[7] However, with respect to art Joyce's eyes seem to have never been clouded by passion. He was sufficiently objective, for instance, to enjoy Aquinas' hymn,

> Pange lingua gloriosi corporis mysterium,

which asserts that though the senses give no evidence of the transubstantiation the pure heart may be assured of it by faith alone—

> et si sensus deficit,
> Ad firmandum cor sincerum sola fides sufficit.[8]

—a way of thinking Joyce despised. "It is an intricate and soothing hymn," says Stephen. "I like it" (*Portrait*, 246). That judgment is purely aesthetic if ever one was. Joyce constantly strove toward the ideal of the impersonal, godlike artist, and found authority for it in the *Summa Theologica*.

What Joyce in the *Portrait* calls desire and loathing (240), Aquinas calls desire and aversion (cf. Aristotle, *Nicomachean Ethics*, VI, 2), and relates them to the concupiscible and irascible powers of the soul; I don't say "respectively," for the relationship is very complex; however, in general the nature of the concupiscible power is to move toward objects of sense or phantasms of imagination for the purpose of possessing them; of the irascible power, to move away from them, or to move toward them for the purpose of destroying them (I, Q. 81, Art. 1). But it is the nature of reason to direct these powers—to move them, not to be moved by them:

For wherever there is order among a number of motive powers, the second only moves by virtue of the first: wherefore the lower appetite is not sufficient to cause movement, unless the higher appetite consents. . . . In this way, therefore, the irascible and concupiscible are subject to reason (I, Q. 81, Art. 3. Cf., however, Aristotle, *De Anima,* III, 10).

They can resist the commands of reason, but this is not to say that they are not subject to it. Reason can cause us, for example, to move away from an object we desire or toward one we loathe; it thus endows us with freedom of action: a sheep runs from a wolf because it must, even if there is no danger, but a man may rationally decide whether he will run or not (I, Q. 81, Art. 3, Reply Obj. 2). In every sense of the term, reason is above desire and loathing; and art, in the aesthetic sense, is addressed to this highest, passive faculty of the soul, for which it is a good (II. I, Q. 32, Art. 8).

Beauty and goodness are fundamentally the same but logically different; for goodness relates to desire but beauty relates to cognition: "That is called good which simply pleases the appetite, but that is called beautiful the mere apprehension of which pleases" (II. I, Q. 27, Art. 1, Reply Obj. 3).[9] Stephen quotes a similar passage: "beautiful things are those which please when seen. Hence beauty consists in due proportion," and our pleasure in beauty comes from our recognition of due proportion (I, Q. 5, Art. 4, Reply Obj. 1; cf. Aristotle, *Metaphysics,* XIII, 3). But perfect pleasure consists in complete possession of, and repose in, the perfectly good (II. I, Q. 33, Art. 2);[10] "and the movement of desire, tending to what was not possessed, ceases" (II. I, Q. 33, Art. 2, Reply Obj. 1).

Thus due proportion and desire are mutually exclusive. Since, moreover, the lower appetites resist the commands of reason (I, Q. 81, Art. 3, Reply Obj. 2) and their motion impedes its operation (II. I, Q. 6, Art. 7, Reply Obj. 3; Q. 9, Art. 2, Reply Obj. 3), a degree of calm is essential for the production and even for the enjoyment of art. The passions belong to the appetitive rather than to the apprehensive part of the soul (II. I, Q. 22, Art. 2). In the presence of a good work of art, says Stephen in the *Portrait,* the soul is "arrested and raised above desire and loathing" (240).

Pornographic and didactic works of art, since they excite desire or loathing, approval or disapproval, are "therefore improper," since the aesthetic emotion is of a radically different nature. The artist's proper business is not that of the sensual man or of the anti-sensual citizen, and the three can hardly understand one another except as they are aware of tendencies shared in common. The sensual man enjoys a picture because it shows him a naked woman; the citizen deplores it for the same reason, but admires another because it depicts a wholesome rural way of life; the artist (as artist) judges both pictures in terms of line, color, composition, and visual insight: he is not at the moment concerned with sex or sociology, but with artistry.

Thus Aquinas' view of art affords a perfect justification for Joyce's refusal to become involved in the distracting enthusiasms of his contemporaries. His ideal of art was more profoundly Catholic than theirs; for by denying to art any moral or social value it would all but destroy art's significance for common life, leaving the field clear to religion and politics. These may indeed use books and pictures, but primarily for purposes of propaganda, not of art. Like jesting Plato, and after him unjesting Tertullian, Augustine, and how many other pious thinkers, Joyce put the artist as such outside the scope of decent (that is, ordinary) human intercourse. Under such conditions the artist, being human, is inevitably "of twosome twiminds"; he is torn between his work and his family, the human family; and to the extent that he devotes himself to his work he is a sinner—in God's eyes, in man's eyes, and in his own.

To choose that way of life, and to persevere in it, requires extraordinary fortitude. This of course no man can give another; certainly it cannot be acquired by reading a book; nevertheless, a book may clarify and confirm our native disposition, and Joyce had authoritative support for his decision to forgo the self-conscious picturesque provincialism of Dublin's literary clique—

> Those souls that hate the strength that mine has
> Steeled in the school of old Aquinas.[11]

Aquinas included in the *Summa Theologica* a treatise of one hundred forty-five pages on fortitude, defining its place among the cardinal virtues, its parts, its operation, its requirements in the way of temperament, the vices opposed to it, and the precepts pertaining to it. Joyce's whole life was a manifestation of this difficult virtue, and the struggles it entailed constitute one of the main themes of his work. Most of the people in *Dubliners* suffer from lack of fortitude; the *Portrait* is a study in the growth of fortitude; in *Ulysses,* fortitude saves Bloom and Stephen Dedalus from the general disintegration; in *Finnegans Wake,* fortitude is the virtue of the devils and lack of fortitude the vice of the angels.

As defined by Aquinas, the essence of fortitude is deliberate choice of a difficult or dangerous course, and perseverance in it. To face a difficulty or danger fearlessly through ignorance, or through confidence born of experience and skill in overcoming it, or through desperation or rage or vainglory, is not fortitude; to face a difficulty or danger which one fears, which one has no experience or skill in overcoming, which one need not face, which one is not expected to face, and which one will get no credit for facing—that is fortitude. (Cf. Aristotle, *Nicomachean Ethics,* III, 6–9.) Its perfect expression is martyrdom, "the most perfect of human acts" (II. II, Q. 124, Art. 3); but since we are not called upon to embrace martyrdom every day, fortitude in daily life "denotes a certain firmness of mind . . . both in doing good and in enduring evil, . . . so as not to forsake the good on account of difficulties, whether in accomplishing an arduous work, or in enduring grievous evil" (II. II, Q. 39, Art. 1). What could better describe Joyce's own character?

The elements of fortitude, says Aquinas (summing up the analyses of Cicero, Macrobius and Aristotle), are magnanimity, magnificence, patience and perseverance (II. II, Q. 129). Opposed to magnanimity are the vices of presumption, ambition, vainglory and pusillanimity; opposed to magnificence is the vice of meanness, and opposed to perseverance are the vices of effeminacy and pertinacity. In Joyce's work the dramatic opposition of these virtues and vices is embodied in the opposition of characters one to another and of conflicting tendencies in individual characters. This does not really violate Joyce's antididactic principle; it illustrates, rather, his principle that the artist's godlike freedom is most fully expressed by the dramatic interplay of characters each endowed with unique qualities and private will (*Portrait,* 252). A dramatic conflict is not primarily a physical conflict; even a barroom fight in a Western movie owes most of its interest to the clash of values implicit in the clash of bodies.[12] We are interested only if we care who wins, and we care only if the outcome makes a difference in terms of our own values. A life-and-death struggle between an octopus and a shark is not very interesting; a fight between an eagle and a snake is interesting because we want the eagle to win. Symbolism is involved here; as the word "interest" implies, we are "in" the fight. For the same reason, a quiet conversation between two men may be very exciting. Neither of the men need be an interesting personality or even an articulate talker; merely as an embodiment of values he has a dramatic or aesthetic interest—not as an allegorical figure, but as a concrete manifestation of certain human tendencies. A process of abstraction takes place here, but with good art the spectator must do his own abstracting. A didactic writer does the job himself, from lack of confidence in the reader or in his own talent, and thereby deprives his work of the liveliness that comes of engaging the reader's imagination. But general ideas there must be, since particulars as such are unintelligible and meaningless. All human life, as J. D. Salinger might say if you held a knife to his throat, is a conflict between two powerful tendencies, love and squalor; and certainly the elements of fortitude are on the side of love, and certainly their contrary vices are on the side of squalor. To portray the clash of values for the sake of its dramatic interest is an artistic activity; didacticism is a different kind of activity, since it contrives a clash to illustrate a point of view and sometimes fakes the values as well. At its worst, it is merely a statement to the effect that a clash is taking place, and what it requires of the reader is not participation but assent. Artistic activity, being concrete and inductive, is apt to be more honest. Propaganda makes poor art for the same reason that it makes poor science and poor philosophy: because it is thinking about something else. It should be added, of course, that this is true only if the requirements of propaganda make the artist neglect or violate the requirements of art. There is a qualitative difference, after all, between *The Brothers Karamazov,* which is full of propaganda, and *In His Steps,* which is *merely* propaganda. We must not say to an artist, "Sing me a song of social significance," but neither must we say to him, "Sing me a song without social significance"; we must leave him alone. He may choose, like George Orwell, to write on political themes; but he should not choose such themes under compulsion or even under pressure, for then he would have to trim his art to fit the message. He may trim it anyhow if he believes a good end can be achieved by bad means. But Joyce was no trimmer; he knew that the end is influenced by the means; he never mortified his art; there was no conflict between his desire to express himself and his decision to write, as he told Grant Richards, a chapter of the moral history of Ireland.[13] In the *Portrait* Stephen says his problem is to hit the conscience of his countrymen, "that they might breed a race less ignoble than their own" (280). This is certainly a nonartistic, even a propagandistic purpose; but it is a purpose quite different from what Buck Mulligan in *Ulysses* mockingly calls "Kalipedia": eugenics and social salvation through the prenatal influences of "genuinely good music, agreeable literature, light philosophy, instructive pictures, plastercast reproductions of classical statues such as Venus and Apollo, [and] artistic coloured photographs of prize babies" (411). Joyce's purpose is one that cannot be achieved by any such false or easy means: people can be lulled into living stupidly, but they cannot be lulled or gulled into living intelligently. Joyce's means, accordingly, are those of an artist, not of an educationist or a public relations expert; his theory of art is concerned entirely with valid means, and is applicable to any content whatever, for his faith is that truth can do no wrong. Let us therefore consider his dramatic treatment of the elements of fortitude and their contrary vices, in the order in which they are discussed by Aquinas; to do this we must summarize Aquinas' analyses.

Magnanimity "by its very name denotes stretching forth of the mind to great things," and the magnanimous man "is minded to do some great act" (II. II, Q. 129, Art. 1). He seeks honor and shuns dishonor—not as external manifestations but as internal dispositions; he seeks, that is, to act greatly if possible, but worthily even in small things—to behave in a way that men should honor, whether they do or not. To the extent that he succeeds, he is independent of the opinion of others and has freedom of action:

> he is not uplifted by great honours, because he does not deem them above him; rather does he despise them, and much more such as are ordinary or little. In like manner he is not cast down by dishonour, but despises it, since he recognizes that he does not deserve it (II. II, Q. 129, Art. 3).

He has much the same attitude toward the material goods of fortune: he despises them in that he feels no need to do anything unbecoming for their sake, but appreciates their usefulness in the accomplishment of his work. Like all the Aristotelian and Thomistic virtues, maganimity is a golden mean, and its contrary vices are extremes.

Presumption, for example, consists in undertaking to do what is beyond one's power through overestimating one's own ability (II. II, Q. 130, Art. 1), or in aspiring to undeserved honors through overestimating one's own worth, or in regarding as virtues such things as one's wealth, good clothes or imperious manner (II. II, Q. 130, Art. 2, Reply Obj. 3). Ambition also is "opposed to magnanimity as the inordinate to that which is well ordered" (II. II, Q. 131, Art. 2); the ambitious man desires "recognition of an excellence which he has not: this is to desire more than his share of honour" (II. II, Q. 131, Art. 1), and he desires it for his own sake rather than for the honor of God or the good of his neighbor. Vainglory is the desire to be honored for things that are not worthy of honor, by people who are not qualified to judge (II. II, Q. 132, Art. 1); since the vainglorious man therefore cares less for truth than for opinion, and "glories in what the magnanimous man thinks little of" (II. II, Q. 132, Art. 2, Replies Objs. 1, 2), the daughters of vainglory are disobedience, boastfulness, hypocrisy, contention, obstinacy, discord, and love of novelties (II. II, Q. 132, Art. 5). Pusillanimity errs on the other side; for just as presumption makes a man try to exceed his capacity or worth, pusillanimity makes him fall short of what he might do (II. II, Q. 133, Art. 1), either through "fear of failure" (II. II, Q. 133, Art. 2) or through "laziness in considering one's own ability" (II. II, Q. 133, Art. 2, Reply Obj. 1); it is, in fact, "a graver sin than presumption, since thereby a man withdraws from good things" (II. II, Q. 133, Art. 2, Reply Obj. 4), whether in accomplishing his work or in maintaining his convictions.

The other elements of fortitude Aquinas treats more briefly. Magnificence is a disposition to undertake great and lofty things for broad and noble purposes and to spare no expense in achieving them (II. II, Q. 134, Art. 2, Reply Obj. 2). For the exercise of this virtue, money is helpful but not essential: "The chief act of virtue is the inward choice, and a virtue may have this without outward fortune: so that even a poor man may be magnificent" (II. II, Q. 134, Art. 3, Reply Obj. 4). A poor man, that is, may perform a small thing magnificently, spending freely the little he has, and a rich man may perform a big thing meanly. Magnificence is a part of fortitude in that it "tends to something arduous and difficult" (II. II, Q. 134, Art. 4), and its contrary vice is meanness, which inclines a man to unnecessarily small undertakings or makes him fall short in great undertakings through reluctance to spend money (II. II, Q. 135, Art. 1). Meanness, however, is also opposed by another vice, wastefulness, which makes a man spend more than his work requires, out of vainglory or some other vice (II. II, Q. 135, Art. 2, Reply Obj. 3).

Patience is the ability to bear evil "without being disturbed by sorrow," so that one will not abandon the good he is pursuing (II. II, Q. 136, Art. 1; Art. 4, Reply Obj. 2). It has no specific contrary vice. Perseverance is the ability "to persist long in something good until it is accomplished" (II. II, Q. 137, Art. 1); more specifically, it is "long persistence in any kind of difficult good" (II. II, Q. 137, Art. 1, Reply Obj. 1), and therefore it is a part of fortitude (II. II, Q. 137, Art. 2). Its contrary vices are effeminacy, which involves shrinking from the good through love of pleasure or fear of pain, difficulty or danger (II. II, Q. 138, Art. 1), and pertinacity, which is a vainglorious persistence beyond all reason or necessity, arising not from firmness of will but from sinful pleasure in a show of specious excellence (II. II, Q. 138, Art. 2).

In addition to the vices which Aquinas lists as specifically opposed to fortitude, he discusses another which Joyce had to fight against and which figures by name in *Ulysses:* "morose delectation" (48). This is the sin of letting the mind dwell on any pleasure for a long time, whether the pleasure itself be sinful or not (II. I, Q. 31, Art. 2, Reply Obj. 2; Q. 74, Art. 6). The meaning of "morose," from the Latin *mora,* "delay," might be more clearly expressed by "lingering." Lingering delectation, then, obviously militates against fortitude.

Joyce's own fortitude is too well known to need discussion here; examples of his magnanimity, magnificence, patience and perseverance will have occurred to every reader, as well as examples of his lapses from virtue. But the dramatic interplay of virtues and vices is clearer in his work than in his life.

The world of *Dubliners* is moribund because most of its people have no fortitude and the few who have are spiritually adrift, wandering lost among the ruins of personality. These few are the child, "I," of the first three stories, Maria of "Clay," and the Misses Morkan and the late Michael Furey of "The Dead."

The Rev. James Flynn of "The Sisters," marked with the nervous trembling of Cain (11, 18) and with something of Cain's unpopularity (9), lacks any touch of the defiance that made Cain creative in human terms; dismissed from the church, he neither begets a son nor builds a city, but retires to a little room behind his sisters' shop and amuses himself by talking of faith, power and mystery to a child (12). The eucharist he constantly takes is High Toast, a brand of snuff; he spills it on his clothes with the trembling hands that have dropped the chalice, and his red bandanna of repentance is "inefficacious" to remove the stains (11). The purpose of snuff, of course, is to excite the flesh and arouse it to a violent reaction, in which we take a corrupt pleasure. The reaction itself is one of rejection; the pleasure is a painful one, akin to that which Aldhelm took in standing neck-deep in icy water [14] or Saint Benedict in rolling naked through the briar patch.[15] But how tame it is by comparison! Father Flynn's vices are pusillanimity, meanness, vainglory and morose delectation; his redeeming grace is hope, not for himself but for the child (8). The child is saved by righteous anger (9) and patience (9, 14).

Leo Dillon of "An Encounter" suffers from pusillanimity (22, 24); the narrator suffers from vainglory (28, 32), disobedience, love of novelties, and effeminacy (22); at the end, however, he is to some extent redeemed by shame and penitence (32). In "Araby" he suffers from vainglory and love of novelties (37) but is saved by anger at himself (41). The young girl of "Eveline" is doomed by pusillanimity (48).

In Jimmy Doyle of "After the Race" all the vices opposed to fortitude are combined. Though not genuinely happy, he is temporarily excited and elated by external things: rapid motion through space, notoriety, and the possession of money (51). This is presumption of the lowest kind. He finds a morose, vainglorious delight in the "nudges and significant looks" of "the profane world" as he passes by (52); by way of ambition he makes a long drunken speech, and thinks it must have been good because his companions applaud loudly (56). He manages to combine wastefulness with meanness: he is going to "stake the greater part of his substance" not on the accomplishment of anything magnificent but on an opportunity to make more money—"pots of money" (52); on the yacht, however, he gambles recklessly and loses heavily, being so drunk that the others have to calculate his I.O.U.'s for him while he pusillanimously worries: "They were devils of fellows but he wished they would stop" (57). His only consolation is the love of novelties: "this was seeing life, at least" (56). A more pitiful prize would be hard to imagine.

Corley of "Two Gallants" combines presumption, vainglory, morose delectation and meanness. He has never got anywhere with girls on his own lower-middle-class level, except one who was promiscuous and later became a prostitute (63); he has no regular employment (61); nevertheless he thinks of himself as "a gay Lothario" because he has succeeded with a few lascivious servant girls (62), and as a well-informed man because he knows a few plainclothes policemen of dubious discretion: "He knew the inner side of all affairs and was fond of delivering final judgments" (61). Currently he is taking a servant girl out to an open field on her days off; he boasts that she pays the tram fare and gives him cigarettes and cigars because she thinks he is "a bit of class," and he intimates that if she becomes pregnant he can easily drop her because he has been too clever to tell her his name (60). As the climax of the story, he makes his prostitution explicit by asking her for money (73). His friend Lenehan, who hopes like a jackal to share in the proceeds, suffers from extreme pusillanimity. He is a parasitical jester, who by keeping up a flow of desperately witty conversation obtains free drinks from his scornful acquaintances and free biscuits from reluctant bartenders (68). Since the thoughtless Corley uses the whole width of the sidewalk to navigate in, Lenehan from time to time skips into the gutter (58, 61); though approaching the age of thirty-one (69), he dresses like an adolescent (59); in a workmen's restaurant he speaks roughly, pushes his cap back on his head and plants his elbows on the table "in order to belie his air of gentility" (69); he ignores being ignored (73). His only ambition is to find a less difficult way to live without working; he would like to have "a good job" (69), but the wish remains as vague as that. In a brief moment of optimism he thinks he "might yet be able to settle down in some snug corner and live happily if he could only come across some good simple-minded girl with a little of the ready" (70). To settle down in some snug corner with a fool for companion: What stretching forth of the mind to great things! What lofty undertaking, for what noble purpose! What firmness in doing good! What dignity! What happiness!

An equally desperate cowering is revealed in "The Boarding House," where a mother sells her daughter to a good simpleminded young man with a snug corner "in a great Catholic winemerchant's office" and "a bit of stuff put by" (79). Having deliberately thrown her daughter in the way of the boarders, waited impatiently for something to develop, and connived in seduction when it came (76), she stands ambitiously forth as a champion of morality and closes the trap on the reluctant young man one beautiful Sunday morning, to the pealing of church bells and the gentle billowing of lace curtains (77). In this as in everything, she acts firmly, energetically and decisively, but for pusillanimous purposes and mean and ignoble ends. Her considerable vitality is wasted because she dares not attempt anything worthy of it. As for the daughter, she lets herself be seduced because she knows her mother is counting on it, though their mutual under-

standing is never put into words (76); her brother Jack, who
had been loudly, spectacularly and vaingloriously offended at a
spoofing remark about her, meanly acquiesces in the whole affair
and drinks to the closing of the deal (83); the seducer, though he
does not love the girl and in fact is ashamed of her ungrammati-
cal speech, marries her for the same reason that he goes to church
though he is an atheist—because he fears he will otherwise lose
his job (80–81). Finally, the priest to whom he confesses the
seduction responds ignobly, drawing out "every ridiculous detail
of the affair" (80). Everyone acts in the smallest possible way; it
is as if there were no generosity of spirit in all Dublin.

The human value of being settled in a snug corner, from
Joyce's point of view, is indicated in the next story, "A Little
Cloud." Little Chandler, having achieved a snug corner through
pusillanimous drudgery, remains "a prisoner for life" (104) to
what he himself calls his "unfortunate timidity" (99). He has
literary tastes but suppresses them for fear of his wife's indifference or scorn (86); he adapts his life rather to her tastes, her
standards, her prim and brainless notions of what is fitting (102).
His respect for public opinion verges on morbidity: he can't even
buy a blouse for his wife without suffering "an agony of nervous-
ness" and blushing with embarrassment (101–102). He feels that
he has potentialities as a poet, and presumptuously blames the
accident of place for their not being realized: "There was no
doubt about it: if you wanted to succeed you had to go away.
You could do nothing in Dublin" (88). Success, in his vainglorious eyes, means the approval of London's hack reviewers (89–90);
on his way to meet Ignatius Gallaher he has a feeble idea for a
poem, but instead of trying to work it out when he is alone he
dreams of running away to London in order to "live bravely like
Gallaher" (103). He gives way to violent impatience, takes it out
on the baby, and responds to his wife's hatred with tears of
remorse (104–105). Nor does Gallaher live bravely. He is a successful yellow journalist who has no desire to be anything else or
do anything better; his chief motive aside from money is love of
novelties—to be always on the go, seeing new places and new
people, and, as a writer, "always to have something new in [his]
stuff" (91). But what stale stuff it is! How dreary are all his
novelties! His interview with Chandler is an orgy of vainglory,

presumption and morose delectation; he intends to go on having a good time in his raffish way until he gets tired or slows down, and then to "marry money" and wind up in a luxurious snug corner (100).

In "Counterparts," Farrington shirks the drudgery of his job and tamely submits to his employer's bullying; when his tongue does accidentally find a heavy, ready-made sarcasm by way of reply, he apologizes abjectly, but afterward boasts of his wit and spirit to his worthless companions. He pawns his watch for drinks, wastes the proceeds swiftly but with mean misgivings, is defeated in a test of strength by a younger man, and when he goes home beats his small son. His whole day is made up of effeminacy, pusillanimity, vainglory, morose delectation, impatience and anger.

James Duffy of "A Painful Case," who, as Marvin Magalaner has so well pointed out, is a partly autobiographical figure,[16] dooms himself to sterility and a woman to death through presumption and pusillanimity. His life is "an adventureless tale" (135) and he declines adventure's gambit (139). Though he considers himself so free of conventional moral notions that "in certain circumstances" he would be capable of robbing the bank where he works (135), actually he is too timid to take a woman when she offers herself. He has the artist's fastidiousness but not his imagination; and his fastidiousness itself is less aesthetic than priggish. There is no richness in his nature; he withdraws from life, for no purpose but to withdraw; like Shaun in *Finnegans Wake,* "He points the deathbone and the quick are still" (193).

The characters of "Ivy Day in the Committee Room" are cursed with all the vices opposed to fortitude. They presumptuously carp against their betters; they effeminately shirk their duty in the present while pertinaciously fighting again the lost battles of the past; they meanly excuse their inactivity by the fact that their promised pay is not forthcoming, but revise their opinion of their candidate upward when he sends them bottles of stout; they are pusillanimously cordial to men whom they revile behind their backs; they vaingloriously assert their own moral and social superiority; they ambitiously maximize the little work they have done, and minimize that of others; and with morose delectation they grow sentimental over the betrayal of Parnell by men like themselves: "Musha, God be with them times! . . . There was some life in it then" (153). If there is no life in it now, it is because no one has Parnell's fortitude.

Mrs. Kearney of "A Mother" is subject to what the young Joyce, in "The Day of the Rabblement," had called "every flattering influence of vanity and low ambition." [17] Her girlish dreams of romance were not of love or art or any kind of service to humanity, but of "a brilliant life" in which her ability to speak French and to play the piano could be turned to social account. Having failed to find a young man with the temperament and the means to give her such a life, she has pusillanimously married a dull but fairly prosperous citizen "much older" than herself and settled down in the snug corner he provides (172). She takes part in the fashionable musical life of Dublin, and when the Irish Revival becomes "appreciable" she decides to "take advantage" of her daughter Kathleen's name and join it. To her, the intellectual awakening of her country is merely an opportunity to extend her social activities. There are Irish lessons and piano lessons for Kathleen, and in the street-corner gossip after mass she is often mentioned as "a very nice girl" (173). When Kathleen is engaged as accompanist for a series of concerts by a musical society, Mrs. Kearney sees it as a social and perhaps matrimonial opportunity justifying a considerable expenditure of time, energy and money: this is presumptuous enough, but when through mismanagement the concerts are poorly attended, her concern for her daughter's fee reveals her basic presumption most clearly: she feels that any abatement of the fee would dishonor her daughter. The others mistake her motive for meanness; she makes such a scene over eight guineas that everyone is disgusted and Kathleen's musical career is finished as far as Dublin is concerned (186). Kathleen, though horribly embarrassed, and though she could simply go out on the stage and play, pusillanimously obeys her mother; and Mr. Kearney, though he remains pusillanimously silent, backs up his wife by his presence, permitting himself to be used for "his abstract value as a male" (179), an act of pure presumption.

Tom Kernan of "Grace" is an unsuccessful businessman who

from time to time escapes into drunkenness. This is effeminacy, an inability to persevere in face of pain or difficulty. He is also presumptuous, since he regards gaiters and a silk hat as essential to his self-respect (195) and professes "a feeling" for the Jesuits because they "cater for the upper classes" (208). His friends share his presumption, admiring the Jesuits for their power and influence: "They're the grandest order in the Church, Tom. . . . The General of the Jesuits stands next to the Pope. . . . They're the boys have influence. . . . Look at their church, too. . . . Look at the congregation they have" (208). One of the friends, Martin Cunningham, vaingloriously speaks in complete ignorance of the subject. The Jesuits were not merely reformed but abolished from 1773 to 1814; Cunningham, however, says, "Every other order of the Church had to be reformed at some time or other but the Jesuit Order was never once reformed. It never fell away. . . . That's a fact. . . . That's history" (208). As might be expected, people who take such a mundane view of religion are spiritually pusillanimous. They plan a retreat with a "fine, jolly fellow" of a priest, who will spare them the depths and the heights of religious experience: "He won't be too hard on us, Tom. . . . He's a man of the world like ourselves" (209). And sure enough, the priest, instead of talking like a spiritual leader, talks like a businessman (222).[18] In view of his authority and the opportunities it gives him, he is the most pusillanimous of them all.

Gabriel Conroy of "The Dead" suffers from presumption, vainglory, ambition, impatience, pertinacity and pusillanimity; he means well, but he is a fatuous windbag. His weakness is overshadowed, however, by the fortitude of the Misses Morkan and of the dead Michael Furey. The three sisters are altogether admirable: they live with zest, vigor and gaiety, and at the same time with dignity, decorum, and a proper sense of their own worth. Their supper party is magnificent in every sense of the word; their music teaching, and their own singing and playing, show the magnanimity of a constant striving for excellence; their patience and perseverance are indicated by the length of their joint career and the incessant work with which they meet the difficulties of their situation. And the dead Michael Furey wears

Summary of character

fortitude's ultimate crown, having died a martyr to a hopeless love. He might have been cautious and lived; he chose instead, though not deliberately seeking death, to risk it in order to express what was in his heart. In these four people fortitude appears as its own reward, giving value to life and death. This story seems to me Joyce's most optimistic work; and beyond the story is Gabriel's journey westward, during which he is to redeem himself by dying for others.[19] He is to become a Christ figure.

In "Clay," however, Maria's fortitude is to no avail; and this story is a more nearly typical expression of the book's prevailing view. Maria is an efficient and respected worker, cheerful, thoughtful of others, generous, kind and even gay—all this while living under conditions that would crush most people and that promise nothing better for the future. Doubtless she has her reward, but it hardly seems worth while; her fortitude will lead to nothing but a charity ward at the end, and her life, potentially so rich, will have been wasted.

As a chapter in the moral history of Ireland, *Dubliners* is an expression of almost absolute pessimism; yet, such is the impersonality of its means, it does not arouse us to want to do anything about the conditions it portrays; it is not a tract or a sermon but a pure work of art made in strict accordance with Aquinas' principles. In *Finnegans Wake* Joyce wrote all history as "one continuous present tense" (185–186); in *Dubliners,* by fixing that single moment through which all future plunges to the past (*Ulysses,* 184), he arrests the soul in the presence of that which is grave and constant in human sufferings and raises it above desire and loathing (*Portrait,* 239–240). This is the tragic pleasure, perhaps the most evil of all pleasures.

In the *Portrait,* a more hopeful book, we see the beginning, growth and development of fortitude as Stephen Dedalus learns to value his own integrity and to estimate his own powers. Its issue is the determination to do a great work despite all obstacles, external and internal. The strength of soul that makes this determination possible is developed from day to day in the exigencies of schoolboy life. The same influences that corrupt others purify him, because he has the initial self-confidence to make his own observations and reject the conventional or malicious or politic interpretations of others. The small, weak, nearsighted boy who suffers from the cold and mud of the soccer field, who fears the flying ball and the trampling feet (3–4), who can be teased and mocked with impunity because he is so unfamiliar with evil he hardly realizes he is being mocked (10), nevertheless has moral courage, and this increases as he becomes conscious of it. When he is punished unjustly he reports it to the head of the school, as a matter of principle—an unprecedented act that arouses the admiration of everyone, including the prefect who has punished him (53–64, 79–80). This is quite a different thing from the pertinacious sullenness of some of his schoolmates, who, meek enough in their own outward behavior and conventional enough in their own beliefs, urge him to disregard a legitimate summons as an affront to his dignity. But he cares little for "such points of honor" (92); his own honor is a personal, not a public matter, and is not concerned with trivialities (93). It is expressed rather in his refusal to deny his literary judgment in order to escape a beating (88–91), in his refusal to sign a fatuous resolution for universal peace (227–232) or join the nationalist movement in order to avoid being misunderstood (236–238), and generally in his refusal to buy friendship, economic security and social approval by concealing his doubts (282) or trimming his beliefs to the popular pattern. These are the negative concomitants of his positive determination to do a great work:

> I will not serve that in which I no longer believe, whether it call itself my home, my fatherland or my church: and I will try to express myself in some mode of life or art as freely and as wholly as I can. . . . I do not fear to be alone or to be spurned for another or to leave whatever I have to leave. And I am not afraid to make a mistake, even a great mistake, a lifelong mistake and perhaps as long as eternity too. . . . I will take the risk (291–292).

He conceives the effort to express himself as a battle and his enemy as Irish provincialism, symbolized by a red-eyed peasant who says, in response to a Dubliner's talk about the stars and the universe, "Ah, there must be terrible queer creatures at the latter

end of the world." Stephen writes in his diary, "I fear him. I fear
his redrimmed horny eyes. It is with him I must struggle all
through this night till day come, till he or I lie dead, gripping
him by the sinewy throat till . . . Till what? Till he yield to
me? No. I mean him no harm" (298). This is the voice of Jacob;
and, like Jacob, Stephen must go into exile. For him, however,
exile is a weapon, since as an artist he must put some moral distance between himself and his subject. To have the detachment
and perspective he needs, especially if he is to work by his own
aesthetic principles, he must live in a different moral atmosphere.
As he tells Davin, the shortest way to Tara is via Holyhead (296)
—that is, via England and the Continent. For the same reason
he must be silent, resisting the temptation to engage in frivolous
polemics at long distance. Both exile and silence are defensive
weapons; the only other weapon he permits himself is cunning,
and this too is hardly offensive. He means no harm to the peasant, who after all is the Angel of the Lord and will of necessity
bless the man who does not yield. He is the artist's material.
Cranly misconstrues "cunning" as intrigue (291); what Stephen
has in mind, however, is not the plotting of a conspirator but
the skill of an artist. It is by developing himself and producing
from himself great works, disregarding all distractions, that he
will hit the conscience of his race. He will do it not by preaching
at them but by facing them with an achievement which they can
ignore only at their spiritual peril.

   The first step in the achievement was *Dubliners;* the second
was the *Portrait;* the third was *Ulysses;* the fourth was *Finnegans
Wake.* If these books are the conscience of Ireland, it is for two
reasons: they are valid as works of art, independently of moral
considerations, and they give expression to the nation's inarticu-
late, subconscious self-knowledge. That is why they have met so
much resistance. They bring forth gods; they create the uncreated.

   In *Ulysses* we follow two men of character through a city of
poltroons—a journey that takes some fortitude on our part as well
as on theirs. During the day Stephen dissociates himself, though
with difficulty, from all the mean influences about him; in the
morning he has companions, a room, a job, and a burden of

remorse; at the end of the night he walks up Eccles Street alone, homeless, companionless and determined to throw up his job, but free at last from any sense of obligation to values other than his own. Bloom wins a victory of a different kind: having re-asserted his Jewishness and his position as master in his own home, he begins to reclaim the personality he has forgone since the death of his son.

Stephen, back in Dublin after a fruitless year in Paris, has an-nounced his intention to write a book in ten years (246). The in-tention, which is ridiculed by Buck Mulligan, recognized briefly and dismissed by Haines, indicates an awareness of the difficulty of his self-imposed task and implies a degree of patience and perseverance highly exceptional in young unpublished writers. Such an intention precludes ambition in the sense in which it is reprobated by Aquinas, since there are easier ways of winning applause; it also precludes vainglory, since no book that takes ten years to write is aimed at the indiscriminate multitude. That the book Dedalus intends is a great one appears from his medita-tions in such varied activities as correcting a child's algebra, walking on the beach, and looking through a lapidary's dusty window. His thoughts are not profound or even original, but they are the *kind* of thoughts that proceed only from genuine magnanimity or greatness of mind, and they are formed with pro-found and original language:

> Across the page the symbols moved in grave morrice, in the mummery of their letters, wearing quaint caps of squares and cubes. Give hands, traverse, bow to partner: so: imps of fancy of the Moors. Gone too from the world, Averroes and Moses Maimonides, dark men in mien and movement, flash-ing in their mocking mirrors the obscure soul of the world, a darkness shining in brightness which brightness could not comprehend (29). . . . Cocklepickers. They waded a little way in the water and, stooping, soused their bags, and, lift-ing them again, waded out. . . . Shouldering their bags they trudged, the red Egyptians. His blued feet out of turnedup trousers slapped the clammy sand, a dull brick muf-fler strangling his unshaven neck. With woman steps she fol-

lowed: the ruffian and his strolling mort. Spoils slung at her
back. Loose sand and shellgrit crusted her bare feet. About
her windraw face her hair trailed. . . . Across the sands of
all the world, followed by the sun's flaming sword, to the
west, trekking to evening lands. She trudges, schlepps, trains,
drags, trascines her load (47–48). . . . Stephen Dedalus
watched through the webbed window the lapidary's fingers
prove a timedulled chain. Dust webbed the window and the
showtrays. Dust darkened the toiling fingers with their vul-
ture nails. Dust slept on dull coils of bronze and silver,
lozenges of cinnabar, on rubies, leprous and winedark stones.
Born all in the dark wormy earth, cold specks of fire,
evil lights shining in the darkness. Where fallen archangels
flung the stars of their brows. Muddy swinesnouts, hands,
root and root, gripe and wrest them. She dances in a foul
gloom where gum burns with garlic. A sailorman, rust-
bearded, sips from a beaker rum and eyes her. A long and
seafed silent rut. She dances, capers, wagging her sowish
haunches and her hips, on her gross belly flapping a ruby
egg (238).

Such thoughts, romantic as they are and ironically as they may be
presented here, nevertheless pursue Blake's ideal: "If the doors
of perception were cleansed every thing would appear to man as
it is, infinite." [20] They comprehend all time, all space, and all
men; they relate the seemingly unrelated, and create the universe of law from the chaos of particulars. To conceive and carry
through an undertaking to organize such thoughts into a work of
art requires great self-confidence. In Chapter II I have indicated
that *Ulysses* shows us Stephen on the climactic day of his liberation from remorse. Remorse may be good for some people sometimes, but for others, especially for artists of independent mind,
it is bad, since for them it militates against magnanimity, magnificence, patience and perseverance. It undermines their moral
position. What we see in *Ulysses*, then, is Stephen struggling toward and finally attaining a moral condition in which the con-
stituent virtues of fortitude will be possible. Such a condition is
in some ways analogous to a state of grace—with this difference,

that it is achieved from within, not conferred from above. It is achieved, accordingly, not by self-surrender but by self-assertion against all odds.

In *Ulysses,* Stephen asserts himself against the whole community in which he lives, enemies and friends alike. He totally disregards his immediate self-interest. Having already written an unfavorable review of a book by Lady Gregory, who got him the part-time post of reviewer and is in a position to help him further (213), he now ignores an invitation to work for the *Evening Telegraph* (133–134), whose editor admires the meretricious cleverness of Ignatius Gallaher (134–136). He also plans to relinquish his teaching job (601), though he is in debt (187) and has no other prospects, because it serves no good purpose and makes no use of his talents. He refuses to make himself agreeable to the literary movement incubating in the National Library, or even to his roommate and his guest, who admire him and would accept him as one of themselves if only he were more tactful and politic, if only he made some effort not to offend with the rebuke of his silence their ways and the world's ways. But his Thomistic honor forbids any such compromise. He deliberately casts off all trivial attachments, thus establishing, as William James would say, at least the negative conditions for the work he will do. Though his intention is not yet clearly defined, his dedication to it leads him to make sacrifices beyond the power of most men. Concomitantly with this magnanimity, within his means he shows a disposition to magnificence—and wastefulness. Shortly after being paid he cautions himself: "By the way go easy with that money like a good young imbecile" (39). He breaks a luncheon appointment with the irresponsible Mulligan and the well-heeled Haines, at which he is expected to pick up the check, but pays to telegraph them an epigram rebuking their meanness: "The sentimentalist is he who would enjoy without incurring the immense debtorship for a thing done" (197). Later he treats the needy Lenehan to a snack (391), stands drinks to the crowd of medical students (417–419), pays the bill for three at the brothel (542–543), and on the way home with Bloom gives half a crown to the importunate Corley (602).

Patience he lacks. He does not suffer fools gladly or bear evil

with equanimity. He is "disturbed by sorrow" to such a degree
that he sinks into drunken delirium, which is certainly not to
his purpose; but even in this degradation he shows a power of
perseverance worthy of his genius and essential to it. As yet his
purpose is only negative, and a negative purpose is harder to
assert and maintain than a positive one; but under the worst
possible conditions he does assert and maintain it. When he is
fagged with debauchery the ghost of his mother rises moldering
from the grave, tells him he too must die, reminds him of his
debt of love to her, urges him to repent, warns him of the fire
of Hell, and prays God to have mercy on him. At first he chokes
with "fright, remorse and horror" (565), but almost immediately
recovers through the action of his wonted intellectual curiosity
and adroitness: "Tell me the word, mother, if you know now.
The word known to all men" (566). When she replies mechani-
cally with the formulas of an orthodoxy in which he no longer
believes, he grows blasphemous and obscene, calling God "the
corpsechewer" and defiantly restating his own position: "With
me all or not at all. *Non serviam!*" The prostitute Florry, who
has noticed how pale he is, rushes out to get him a drink of
water (thus Joyce tips his hat to the tradition of the kind-hearted
prostitute, which goes back at least to Mary Magdalen), and his
anguished mother begs the Sacred Heart of Jesus to save him
from Hell; she identifies herself with Christ, who died and was
transmogrified into Mother Church; but Stephen will not consent to be served or saved, since such consent would involve an
acceptance of values which he does not accept: "No! No! No!
Break my spirit all of you if you can! I'll bring you all to heel!"
He will not take communion at the hands of a prostitute. His
final word is *"Nothung!"*—"Beware!"—as with Siegfried's spear
he smashes the nothing-light of the brothel world (567).

That this is more than a merely impulsive act, that it expresses
a deep conviction as to his own position in the universe, is indicated by his thoughts near the powerhouse in the middle of the
afternoon: "Between two roaring worlds where they swirl, I.
Shatter them one and both. But stun myself too in the blow.
Shatter me you who can" (238). At the end of the day too, "He re-
affirmed his significance as . . . a conscious rational reagent be-

tween a micro- and a macrocosm" (682). The two worlds he is
between are not primarily those of Matthew Arnold; that is to
say, they are not primarily the old Ireland which is dying and
the new Ireland which he correctly foresees will be stillborn;
they are rather the outer and the inner worlds, the dynamo and
the blood that worships the Virgin Mother, the throb of ambition urging him to be on, the pulse of the affects bidding him
stay. In order to accomplish the work he plans, he must assert
his independence of both worlds; the episodes of the novel that
deal with him recount his daylong effort to make that assertion,
to reaffirm himself as "a conscious rational animal proceeding
syllogistically from the known to the unknown" (682), to put his
own reason and his own intuitive insight above the dicta of authority, of ambition, and of blind impulse. He is sure of his own
genius. To Bloom's assurance that Dedalus with his brain and
the peasant with his brawn both belong to Ireland and are
equally important, Dedalus replies, "You suspect . . . that I
may be important because I belong to . . . Ireland. . . . But I
suspect . . . that Ireland must be important because it belongs
to me" (629). This is Ockhamist nominalism carried to its ultimate extreme in twentieth-century individualism, the direct opposite of Thomist orthodoxy.

Bloom does not understand this attitude; nevertheless, he too
is a thinker, since he generalizes and tries to derive principles
from the most commonplace particulars. Throwing a crumpled
handbill into the river, he thinks of the law of falling bodies
(150); going to lunch, he is reminded of the law of the jungle,
communal equality, vegetarianism, cannibalism, and the accident theory of history: "Peace and war depend on some fellow's
digestion" (168–169). Listening to a garrulous sailor, he thinks of
"the enormous dimensions of the waters of the globe," the causes
of wanderlust, and the reputed mystery of the sea, which he
doubts (614). A discussion of prostitution leads him to ontology
(617), and the events of the evening seem to him "a miniature
cameo of the world we live in" (631). His language is vulgar, but
he has a historical sense which professed students of history lack
(226–228).

Morally also he towers above his enemies, though outwardly

they win every encounter. The unique quality by virtue of which he is superior is kindness: he has a genius for being kind. He is wholly without rancor; notwithstanding all his vices and perversions, his view of the world is disinterested: "he desired to amend many social conditions, the product of inequality and avarice and international animosity" (681). This is more than a merely abstract philanthropy; it springs from an instinctive good will toward individuals. Even to the filthy Bantam Lyons, whom he is glad to get rid of, he silently wishes good luck: "God speed scut" (84). Toward those who thwart, slight, snub, contemn or abuse him he feels contempt, disapproval or pity, but never hatred. He feels, though he does not articulate it as a thought, that by offending his individuality they damage their own. The idea of revenge never occurs to him, because he never operates on their level or thinks in their terms. To John Henry Menton, who he knows has always hated him, he is spontaneously courteous and receives in return a cold stare; and notwithstanding a lifetime of experience with such people, he believes that Menton will "be sorry after perhaps when it dawns on him" (114). He cannot conceive that it will not dawn. The practical consideration, "Get the pull over him that way," is an afterthought. Cashel Boyle O'Connor etc. Farrell bumps into the blind piano tuner, almost knocks his cane from his hand, and hurries on without a word of apology or a look of concern (246); Bloom helps the piano tuner across the street, taking care not to "do the condescending" (178), meditates sympathetically on what he must think and feel, and considers the lot of blind people generally: "Terrible. Really terrible. . . . Where is the justice being born that way" (180). He sympathizes with tired horses (75, 178, 646), feeds seagulls (151), and pities a ragged child (150). He contributes generously to the fund for Mrs. Dignam (242) and takes advantage of the letter of the law in her behalf (277, 307-308)—the same letter that Ben Dollard uses in behalf of Father Cowley (242), the difference being that Dollard's purpose is partly malicious and Bloom's is wholly kind.

Such a disposition is liable to arouse the contempt of those who, since they don't share it, can't understand it; certainly it is a disadvantage in business, where to be disinterested is to get left; and in personal relations with naturally vicious people it is disastrous. Bloom's failure is largely due to the fact that he tries to appeal to the better nature of people who have no better nature. He is no more bold than he is truculent; he never provokes conflict with others, and swallows all sorts of insults to avoid it; but when he is directly challenged, intellectually or morally, on his own behalf or on behalf of others, he does not yield. Both with The Citizen (335–339) and with Bella Cohen (568–570), he stands his ground and rebukes his enemy, one for his presumption and pertinacity, the other for her presumption and meanness; in each case he is factual and contemptuous rather than angry, and thus wins a moral victory over his raging enemy. He does not flee from The Citizen but is hurried off by his friends, and even then, since the car is delayed by the crowd, he insists on making his point despite the manifest danger of physical violence; as the car drives away he is still remonstrating with Cyclops. Neither does he flee from Bella Cohen's, but when he hears Zoe say, "There's a row on," he breaks off his remonstrances with the enraged Bella and rushes out to help Stephen, pausing only to throw a shilling on the table for the sixpenny lamp Stephen has broken. In each case he is beset by a hostile public: outside Kiernan's pub by "all the ragamuffins and sluts of the nation" (336) and outside Bella Cohen's by "the hue and cry" of his own guilty conscience (571); the former he ignores, the latter he flees, but seeing the actual crowd around Stephen he recovers his objectivity, elbows through them and takes command of the situation.

Stephen, characteristically, is not interested in being rescued; the two soldiers with whom he is incoherently arguing offer to beat him up, and all Stephen's other friends desert him, but Bloom stands by him, and finally, with Corny Kelleher's assistance, gets him away. Throughout the episode, Bloom's behavior toward the actualities of the outer world is brave and disinterested: intuitively sensing Stephen's unique possibilities, he takes upon himself the noble and arduous task of saving him, and persists in it under the most unfavorable circumstances, chiefly Stephen's own self-destructive tendencies, and against the most wearing difficulties, chiefly a neurotic doubt of his own worthi-

ness and a neurotic self-destructive urge to degrade himself out
of existence. His magnanimity, patience and perseverance overcome all difficulties and all terrors; he also demonstrates what
Saint Thomas calls the inner disposition to magnificence, since
throughout the day, though he is hardly making a living, when
money is called for he pays or gives generously without thinking
about it. He is also pleased by the apparent good fortune of
others, even those he despises. He erroneously thinks that Bantam Lyons, to whom he gave the *Freeman's Journal* he was about
to throw away, has bet on Throwaway and profited accordingly.

> His mood?
> He had not risked, he did not expect, he had not been
> disappointed, he was satisfied.
> What satisfied him?
> To have sustained no positive loss. To have brought a
> positive gain to others. Light to the gentiles (660).

This mood is in sharp contrast to the disappointment, envy and
anger of everyone else involved in the Throwaway contretemps
(329–332, 335); the dry humor inherent in identifying himself
with Saint Paul, and Pauline Christianity with financially profit-
able information, is in sharp contrast to the heavy rancor of his
associates, who in one way or another reject whatever light is
offered. Lyons, having got what he considered a tip from Bloom
(84), rejects it in favor of another from the shiftless Lenehan
(329).

The bettors resent Bloom's supposed secret wealth, and construe his not buying a round of drinks as meanness: "Mean
bloody scut" (335). Though they have been slandering him in
his absence, when he reappears they childishly wish he would
treat them; their only principle is to get whatever they can. He
is superior to them all; as the book proceeds, this unprepossess-
ing, unsuccessful, unrespected, neurotic, guilty, nasty man grows
on us as a moral giant. That is the miracle of *Ulysses*.

No man can look on naked divinity and live: there is the well-
known case of Actaeon, as well as the authority of Scripture;
divinity therefore appears to our weak sight disguised as a

familiar or even a ridiculous object: a bull, a swan, a cloud, a pile of coins, a wrestler, a burning bush, a swineherd, one's own husband, a destitute couple, a carpenter's son—why not an ad salesman? Bloom is the conscience not only of Ireland but of the world. To create him, under all the difficulties that beset Joyce from 1914 to 1921, was an act not only of genius but of the utmost fortitude.

The writing of *Finnegans Wake* was perhaps even more so; for though Joyce's financial and professional position was much improved during the years 1922–1939, his sight deteriorated badly, the work itself was the most difficult any writer had ever undertaken, and the reception he might expect for it was the least promising. Throughout the book, in the relations of Shem and Shaun, he dramatizes his own conception of the relations between himself and the rest of the literary world: the publishers, the journalists, the critics, the professors, the various overlapping reading publics, and the nonreading public that gets its ideas and information from the radio, the movies and the vaudeville stage—all of whom, however remotely, influence the writer's life and work. In only one way can a writer effectively maintain his position vis-à-vis this world: not by punching his enemies in the nose, not by political activity, not by moral campaigning, not by educational or public relations work for any cause however good, but only by writing as well as he can. For a writer as writer, action is something to observe, understand and use, not to participate in; this involves a kind of exile from human affairs, a kind of renunciation of the world, even a kind of immorality —and this was the hard course Joyce undertook. In the *Portrait,* the only weapons Stephen will permit himself are "silence, exile and cunning" (291); in *Ulysses,* challenged to fight by Private Carr, he says, "Personally, I detest action" (573); in the Burrus and Caseous episode of *Finnegans Wake,* Careous Caseous (Shem, Joyce) combines Stephen's world-shattering defiance with his refusal to take direct action: "I'll beat you so lon. (Bigtempered. Why not take direct action. See previous reply)" (167). "Bigtempered" means "magnanimous"; "so lon" means "so long" or "in time," and also "Solon." The classic lawgiver exhorted young men to live and die for their country, and to honor its religion;

he disfranchised those who, like Joyce, were neutral in times of
sedition, and observed that the ruler of a city cannot consider
anything which is to his city's advantage morally wrong. Against
this conception of the overriding importance of the community,
Caseous asserts the artist's individual right to seek or create law
through his art—in his own case, the law of language, the Word.
He prosecutes this impersonal work with religious intensity. For
orthodox Catholics the Word is the Logos, the Idea, the Form
of Forms, God; for Caseous the Word is language, speech, articu-
lacy, thought, individuality, through which alone God is created
and manifested as Law; for both, the Word is the spouse of the
soul, but the two spouses are quite different:

> My unchanging Word is sacred. The word is my Wife. . . .
> The ring man in the rong shop but the rite words by the
> rote order! *Ubi lingua nuncupassit, ibi fas! Adversus hostem
> semper sac!* [Where the tongue speaks, there is law! Against
> the enemy, always justice!] [21] . . . That mon that hoth no
> moses in his sole [no law in his individual makeup, no mazes
> in his dirty soul] nor is not awed by conquists of word's
> law . . .

though he were my brother, says Caseous, is my enemy. And to
the questions, "Are you holy? Are you accursed?" he replies, "We
are Shem" (167–168).

Burrus agrees. From his "acropoll," his pointed head, his high
city ruled by popular vote, he denounces Caseous as

> a boosted blasted bleating blatant bloaten blasphorous bles-
> phorous idiot who kennot tail [Cainnot tell] a bomb from
> a painapple [hand grenade] . . . and wannot psing his
> psalmen with the cong in our [congener] gregational pom-
> poms [massed guns] with the canting [singing, back-slapping,
> begging, cheating] crew (167).

That is to say, he will neither fight nor pray nor join the party:
he will not serve what he no longer believes in. He will serve
only his art, in his own way.

Does this make him an admirable person? Certainly not from society's point of view, and not necessarily from Joyce's own; for the description of Shem and his habits, following immediately after the Burrus and Caseous episode, portrays a person whose only virtue is a fanatic devotion to his work: Shem is a dirty, cowardly, lecherous, drunken, fawning, boring, stinking, conceited, insincere, irresponsible, impious writer of obscenities (170–186). Implicit in the description are great artistic skill and great fortitude, but, since Shem is always seen through the eyes of Shaun, his virtues are never explicitly recognized. Shaun always tells more than he knows. Shem's worst fault, in Shaun's eyes, is his self-confidence in the face of all these facts: "Would anyone, short of a madhouse, believe it? Neither of those clean little cherubum, Nero or Nobookisonester himself, ever nursed such a spoiled opinion of his monstrous marvellosity as did this mental and moral defective (here perhaps at the vanessance [vanishing point] of his lownest)" (177). Thus Joyce describes himself or his ideal of himself, with wild humor and from the point of view of his enemies, but nevertheless in terms that must appall any reasonably social-minded person.

Doubtless he exaggerates; certainly he laughs at his enemies as well as at himself, and assuredly they come off worse than he; but after every possible allowance has been allowed, the artist as here portrayed is still not a good citizen, a reliable associate, a pleasant companion, or even a tolerable person to have around. He knows he isn't, and suffers from the knowledge; he knows also that being an undesirable person does not make him an artist; but Joyce's point is that since Shem's work is great his personal faults are irrelevant, and further that since the artist is by definition original it is inevitable that ordinary people find him strange, insincere and all the rest. That is the risk any man must take who sets out to be an artist—and he has no external assurance that he will be a great one. This is Joyce's apologia; it is a statement, in different form, of the aesthetics he outlined in the *Portrait* and called "applied Aquinas"; it is an expression of the fortitude with which an outcast Irishman, superstitious, neurotic, poverty-stricken, beset by enemies and almost blind, produced serene and noble works of art.

Personal Postscript

There is no necessary relationship between a man's aesthetic theory and the quality of his artistic performance. The fact that Joyce was a great artist does not make his aesthetic theory true; it was not his acceptance of Aquinas' ideas that made him a master of language or gave him the ability to create characters or lit up his apocalyptic vision. In fact, his acceptance with regard to art of a belief in the discontinuity of the outer and the inner worlds, between matter and soul, is inconsistent with his belief in the essential unity of the human personality and his opposition to those who by splitting it justify neglect of the concrete situation in favor of an abstract good never to be realized in anyone's lifetime.

The theory, being Platonic, is the statement of an ideal rather than a description of what actually takes place in aesthetic apprehension: the artist's task, says Stephen in the *Portrait,* is "to express . . . from sound and shape and colour which are the prison gates of our soul, an image of the beauty we have come to understand" (242). Such beauty is ideally perfect because it is purely abstract: its "necessary qualities," which make it universal and independent of local, temporal and personal differences, are merely "certain relations" (245). Thus all art is ideally of the nature of geometry. To Lynch, who has written his name in pencil on the backside of the Venus of Praxiteles (240), Stephen says, "You would not write your name in pencil across the hypothenuse of a rightangled triangle." "No," says Lynch, "give me the hypothenuse of the Venus of Praxiteles" (243). The implication is that Lynch is so insensitive, so hopelessly imprisoned in sound and shape and color, that he is incapable of seeing in any beautiful object the formal relations which alone make it beautiful: the relation "of part to part in any esthetic whole or of an esthetic whole to its part or parts or of any part to the esthetic whole of which it is a part" (241). He is aware only of the concrete object, in its totality and with all its nonartistic associations—or rather, he is not aware of it but responds to it as a leaf turns to the sun or the male to the female. Anything that requires a more complex or subtle response gets none from him. To him, the pubic triangle is beautiful not because of its trigonometric relations but because of its sexual associations— not as an abstract design either visible or intelligible, but as an object of desire; and though Stephen is correct in saying that Lynch's reaction is not "an esthetic stasis" but "simply a reflex action of the nerves" (241),[22] which "leads to eugenics rather than esthetic" (244), the fact remains that not only Lynch but any man is likely to have the same reaction; to call it "kinetic" rather than "aesthetic" is not only to make a merely verbal split in an integral experience but to make the enjoyment of beauty nothing but an intellectual game. Joyce's argument, as the logicians would say, is valid but not true: it is internally consistent but does not conform to the facts, for not even in his own case was the enjoyment of beauty so limited. His theory of art, which was classic and ascetic, denied his own aesthetic experience, which was largely romantic and integrated with his total enjoyment of life.

From the falsity of his theory arises another difficulty for any man of humane impulses. If we cannot truly separate art from the rest of life, we cannot with any consistency ignore the problem of the artist's intention. Is the only legitimate question to ask about a rack, an iron maiden, a whip or a crematorium how well it works? If it works well must we admire it? May we not question its purpose? It is not, like Aquinas' knife, morally neutral. Can we then be morally neutral about it? Oscar Wilde was of course right: the fact that a man is a poisoner is nothing against his prose—but if the prose itself causes people to be killed or stunted, that is something against it. If a poem encourages anti-Semitism, now that we have had a twentieth-century example of what anti-Semitism has always led to, must we confine our criticism to its form? Must we praise a pyromaniac for the skill with which he operates? If a poet loads his poem with propaganda, can he with any grace ask us to read it as if it contained none? That is disingenuous.

In our own time, such disingenuousness is bad not only for people but even for art. Good art is produced only by individuals; each tries to give form to his own vision, and all good art

is private. This was true even in the Middle Ages, when individuality was not highly regarded, most artists were anonymous, and
the greatest works of art were cathedrals built by collective
effort. Every cathedral was full of individual, private touches.
But where the individual is systematically and efficiently forbidden to express his own vision, or where his design must be
approved by a committee of earnest citizens who know what they
are supposed to like, we get the kind of grandiose but lifeless
official art that came from Nazi Germany, that still comes from
Soviet Russia, and that adorns our own parks and public buildings. (O Justice! O Agriculture! O Physical Ed! O Lenin! O
Robert Fulton!) The tendency of much politically motivated
art today (such as Pound's and Eliot's) is to depreciate the individual and to promote a way of life in which, as in the ironical
Plato's Republic, all art would be made according to official
rules laid down by the public guardians of morality.[23] But we
cannot avoid censorship by censoring artists—or critics. No artist
should be forbidden to express his prejudices; but neither should
criticism be inhibited by a priggishly narrow definition of art.
That too is a form of censorship.

CHAPTER VIII

The Godlike Artist: Augustine Again

To God all things are beautiful and good and just, but men have always considered some things just and some unjust.—Heraclitus, Fragment 102.

SAINT AUGUSTINE, WHOSE NAME JOYCE BORE WITHIN HIS OWN, WAS partly responsible for the dramatistic theory of art set forth in the *Portrait* and followed to a greater or less degree in all Joyce's works. He was also partly responsible for Joyce's theory of the godlike artist, and perhaps to some extent even for his conviction of the irrelevance of moral standards to artistic judgment. The three ideas are all of a piece, each supporting and supported by the others, in Augustine's theodicy as in Joyce's aesthetics. This is not to say that Joyce was an Augustinian, except in the sense that, being preoccupied with the ideas we most strongly oppose, we are willy-nilly influenced by them; in the same way that Augustine turned the devices of pagan rhetoric "to a Christian use" and made them "fight for truth," [1] Joyce turned certain Augustinian notions to the service and defense of art.

Genius has little reverence for ideas. It uses them. Joyce used Augustine and the whole classic tradition for new purposes. Plato's ironic suggestion that the arts and sciences were properly subordinate to politics became among Christian thinkers the earnest belief that they were properly handmaids of theology; not until Joyce did any artist dare to "kill the priest and the king" within himself (*Ulysses*, 574), to regard both politics and theology as nothing more than materials for art, and to subordinate both church and state to the personality of the artist. "You

Notes to Chapter VIII begin on page 159.

die for your country, suppose," says Stephen Dedalus to the British soldiers. "Not that I wish it for you. But I say: Let my country die for me" (576). And to Bloom he says, "You suspect . . . that I may be important because I belong to the *faubourg Saint-Patrice* [that suburb of the church] called Ireland for short. . . . But I suspect . . . that Ireland must be important because it belongs to me" (629). The same notion appears in *Stephen Hero* (246). In the *Portrait,* announcing his artistic intention, he asserts that he will try to fly by means of the nets that have been flung at him—the nets of nationality, language and religion (238). Certainly Joyce was aided in his flight by the net of Augustinian theodicy.

Augustine worked in the shadow of Tertullian by the light of Cicero and Quintilian. Though he had the best education the age afforded, though he was the master of an ornately beautiful Latin style and (to his sorrow) never lost his pagan delight in a well-turned sentence, he did not approve of secular learning or literary art except as means of propagating the faith. The roots of his attitude were in the classic tradition itself. Under the dictatorship of Julius Caesar, when thoughtful public discussion was penalized, when fools orated and wise men stayed at home, when rhetoric had no content and wisdom no tongue, Cicero set forth a regime of education for the man who he hoped would one day restore republican liberty—the informed and intelligent speaker, the *doctus orator,* no philosopher king but a private citizen willing to speak out for the public good and able to speak effectively.[2] Quintilian—for whom, as a Stoic, virtue was an end in itself and outward circumstances could not be helped—was less interested in promoting liberty than in persuading individuals to amend their lives. At his hands, therefore, the ideal of the informed speaker was transmogrified into that of the good man skilled in speaking—Cato's *vir bonus dicendi peritus.*[3]

Quintilian's *Institutio Oratoria,* the fruit of twenty years of teaching, had a strong effect on such early Christian thinkers as were not absolutely opposed to the reading of pagan books, notably on Saint Augustine, who in any case had read it before his conversion. From the good man skilled in speaking it was an easy transition to the Christian skilled in teaching, the ideal of

De Doctrina Christiana.[4] That was a considerable advance over
the attitude of Tertullian, who (having a magnificently developed *odium theologicum*) had written, "What has Jerusalem to
do with Athens? Or the Church with the Academy? Or Christians
with heretics? . . . We who have Christ Jesus need no curiosity;
we who have the Gospel need no investigation." [5] But Saint Augustine, who was concerned to explain the fact of evil in a world
made by a good and omnipotent God, took a more liberal attitude: "Let everyone who is a good and true Christian know that
truth is the truth of his Lord, wheresoever it be found"; since the
liberal arts developed by the pagans are "better suited to the
service of truth," and since even pagan philosophy contains
truths that support the faith, Christians should take such arts
and truths from their "wrongful possessors" [6] and use them "for
the confuting of heretics." [7]

Augustine's specific use of them was to justify God's ways by
portraying Him as an artist—a conception that profoundly influenced Joyce's view of himself as artist and of the creative process. Though it is wicked to study music for its own sake, said
Augustine, we can learn from it what great souls learn by flights
of intuition: that in nature, as in a perfect poem, nothing is accidental or unintended; that just as a syllable may be replaced by
an interval of silence, or a long syllable by two short ones or by
a short one and a rest, and the whole poem gain in artistic interest by the variations thus achieved within a single rhythmic
pattern, so all seeming inequalities, whether of the stars in their
courses or of human beings in theirs, "join in melodious succession, as it were in a song of the universe." [8] Let us not complain
if it falls to our lot to be a short syllable or even a rest. If we
cannot apprehend the harmony, the order, the justice of the
whole and of our position in it, neither can a statue in an outer
niche of a building see the whole building, or a soldier in the
front line of battle the disposition of the whole army. We are
disposed in the order of things according to our merit as pre-
determined by God's will, "not knowing what beauty divine
providence will bring forth by means of us." If, for example,
God ordains us to have a wicked will and violate His law, and
then punishes us for violating it, that is not wicked of Him: He

does it only in order that the punishment of our imperfection
may fulfill the law and demonstrate its perfection. Thus God's
good works subsist even in man's bad works.[9]

This notion is developed more fully in the *Enchiridion*. Since
nothing happens against God's will; since even when the wicked,
"as far as they themselves are concerned," act against His will,
His will concerning them is thereby fulfilled; since "as far as
His omnipotence is concerned" they do His will by opposing it;
since He thus achieves His good purposes "through the evil wills
of evil men," [10] it follows that the individual is of no consequence
or value as such but only as part of the grand design. In his
polemic *Against the So-Called Fundamental Letter of Mani-
chaeus*, Augustine states this clearly and justifies it in terms of
God's artistry:

> Just as the utterance of the voice passes away and perishes
> in silence, and yet our speech is formed by the departure
> and succession of passing words, and is properly and pleas-
> antly divided by intervals of silence, so likewise the humble
> beauty of temporal natures is formed and made distinct by
> the passing away of things and the death of those born.[11]

Their beauty, that is, inheres less in themselves than in their
relationships and the patterns to which they contribute. The
same notion appears in *De Musica:* since the perfection of a
poem requires that the individual syllables pass away, and since
man is an instrument of God's will as a syllable is an instrument
of the poet's will, "God, supremely good and supremely just,
grudges no beauty, whether it be achieved by the soul's damnation, or retreat, or endurance." [12] Evil being a merely negative
condition, an absence or deficiency of good, the function of the
evil man in God's work is analogous to that of a rest in music.
Thus does God compose the poem of the universe without regard
to man's limited and self-interested notions of right and wrong.
God is an artist, not a humanitarian. Augustine says specifically, quoting Romans 9:11–21, that we are not qualified to
impugn His justice.[13]

It hardly needs saying that such a God is not understandable in human terms; that is one of the central doctrines of Augustine's Neo-Platonic Christianity. Rare spirits at rare moments have had glimpses of the inexplicable splendor, but their efforts to communicate the experience to us who are more grossly made or less finely tuned are never quite successful; they all have reason to complain with Richard Rolle that we understand the verses of their song but not the song of their verses.[14] Joyce had more natural piety than most of us, and in the *Portrait* Stephen once experiences the mystic union, "the ecstasy of seraphic life" (255). But the experience takes place in a dream, and is never repeated in any waking hour. The child who can "encounter reality" only through imaginary participation in formal religious rites (184) becomes a youth who can encounter it only through art (299). But the need to encounter it remains unchanged. Stephen recalls how one evening

> he had dismounted from a borrowed creaking bicycle to pray to God in a wood near Malahide. He had lifted up his arms and spoken in ecstasy to the sombre nave of trees, knowing that he stood on holy ground and in a holy hour. And when two constabulary men had come into sight round a bend in the gloomy road he had broken off his prayer to whistle loudly an air from the last pantomime (273).

The disposition that led to such a moment, however, was forced to find a different mode of expression. There were too many constables in Joyce's own mind. There was Moynihan, for example, speaking of ellipsoidal balls (224, 256); there was the unjust Father Dolan (53–56); there was the Church itself, in the person of the Rector, tempting him with power as Satan had tempted Christ (182–86). Thus Joyce faced the dilemma every intellectual with a strong religious impulse must face, but his solution was the opposite of the mystics'. They disavow reason; he disavowed faith. It was difficult. "I am a product of Catholicism," said the hero of *Stephen Hero;* ". . . I cannot in a moment destroy every feeling in my nature. That takes time" (139). It took his whole life. Joyce never destroyed his native piety to such an extent that he could ignore it. Like the reformed drunkard who, lacking a normal ability to take it or leave it, regards alcohol with a horror as obsessive as his former craving, Joyce could never be indifferent to religion. He fought it all his life, as for some years he fought a tendency to drink too much, and for essentially the same reason. The slogan "Guinness is good for you" rings throughout *Finnegans Wake,* always in the same ironical tone as do certain formulas of piety, "Hail, Mary, full of grace," "Holy Mary, Mother of God," "The Father, the Son and the Holy Ghost," "Matthew, Mark, Luke and John," and Augustine's joyful cry of amazement, "O felix culpa!" The mystical consciousness, says William James, like the drunken consciousness, rises above "the cold facts and dry criticisms of the sober hour. Sobriety diminishes, discriminates, and says no; drunkenness expands, unites, and says yes." [15] Stephen's conversation was full of cold facts and dry criticisms because Joyce needed them. They were an antidote not only to his companions' muddleheadedness but to his own mystical tendencies. Every writer, in order to compose in tranquillity, must get above his material, diminish it, discriminate, and say no; for Joyce especially this was an absolute necessity, since when he worked he consciously imitated Augustine's God.

The side of his aesthetic that he got from Aquinas emphasized the irrelevance of nonartistic standards in judging works of art; the side that he got from Augustine emphasized the irrelevance of nonartistic standards in creating works of art. From Aquinas he learned to see, through the accidents of sound and shape and color (*Portrait,* 242), the formal relations (241) which are "the essence of beauty" (205). From Augustine he learned not to distort such relations by bending them to human requirements, political, moral or emotional. Just as Augustine denies that God can be understood in terms of human morality, so Stephen denies that art can be either created or understood in terms of values other than its own:

> Our flesh shrinks from what it dreads and responds to the stimulus of what it desires by a purely reflex action of the nervous system. . . . Beauty expressed by the artist cannot awaken in us an emotion which is kinetic or a sensation

which is purely physical. It awakens, or ought to awaken, or induces, or ought to induce, an esthetic stasis, an ideal pity or an ideal terror (241).

The ideal is almost mathematical in its purity. The highest form of art, the dramatic, is not merely a reproduction of life, but "life purified and reprojected from the human imagination" (252), the function of the imagination being to work the raw material of life into "the most satisfying relations of the sensible" and "of the intelligible" (243).

The most important words here are "purified" and "ideal." They are the keys to Joyce's intention. Stephen is careful to distinguish between the uses of words "in the literary tradition," which has nothing to do with current practicalities, and "in the marketplace" (219, 250); in the marketplace their purity of meaning is compromised by the immediate human context—when the word "detain" is adapted to the practical considerations of the moment it loses something of its essential or ideal meaning (219), and the word "beauty" as used in the marketplace loses its "wider sense" (250). The uses of the marketplace, that is to say, are rough and inaccurate, and therefore unsuited to the requirements of art. The dean of studies uses the vague language of the marketplace, calling a tundish a funnel, and Stephen makes bold to correct him (219–220, 297). A tundish is a particular kind of funnel; when Stephen, to make himself understood, has to use the merely generic term, he does so reluctantly. Call this pedantry if you will. He takes unfavorable notice of Cranly's using the word "eke" for "e'en" (238, 281), is irritated when McCann calls him "a reactionary" because he will not sign a resolution for universal peace sponsored by the Czar of Russia (231), and is disheartened by the "sour smelling" question, "What then is your point of view?" (291). In one of his early book reviews Joyce chided an author who used the word "certainty" for "certitude." [16]

Stephen too, requiring precision of thought and speech, cultivates it in himself, for if he is to purify life he must have a pure medium. He must divorce his speech from the common speech of men. He must be able to report their speech accurately in all its inaccuracy, but if he is to do anything more, if he is to express beauty from such "sluggish matter" (196), such "lumps of earth" (221), "the gross earth or what it brings forth" (242), "the daily bread of experience" (260), "the reality of existence" (299), he must command a fine instrument, "a lucid supple periodic prose" (194). The beauty of literature thus inheres not in the material but in the art of writing; what Stephen chiefly likes about words is "the poise and balance of the period itself," and what he most enjoys about writing is not "the reflection of the glowing sensible world through the prism of a language many-coloured and richly storied," not language's "associations of legend and colour," not even his own "inner world of individual emotions"—not any subject matter—but the contemplation of the inner world "mirrored perfectly": the contemplation of his own artistry (193–194). The opening chapter of Genesis is punctuated with the joyful refrain, "And God saw that it was good." Augustine's whole conception of God as artist is a development of that theme, and Joyce's conception of drama as the highest form of literature follows Augustine as well as Aristotle.

Literature, says Stephen, is "the highest and most spiritual form of art." Even in its simplest form—the "rhythmical cry" that constitutes a lyric expressing an instant of emotion—the artist begins to rise above himself, since he is "more conscious of the instant of emotion than of himself as feeling emotion" (251). This is a fair description of the *Portrait,* an essentially lyrical utterance, though, as Stephen admits, the forms are often blended and confused. From the lyric emerges the simplest form of the epic, in which "the narrative is no longer purely personal," since "the personality of the artist passes into the narration itself" in which the characters and the action are bathed as in "a vital sea." This is a fair description of *Ulysses.* The narrative is no longer purely personal, since the author, though he is the central character, is no longer the only character. Being involved with others, he necessarily regards them with interest and thereby attains a greater distance from himself. In the *Portrait* the other characters serve merely as background for Stephen; they are seen only through his eyes, and they talk only that he may reply or react; there is no scene in which he is not the central figure.

Ulysses is a different matter. Here the artist is concerned primarily with art and only incidentally with his personal emotions. He achieves the dramatic form, however, only when he can develop a story independently of his own feelings and attitudes; when, regarding life like Stephen Hero with a "remorseless lack of sentiment for himself no less than for others" (151), he can use characters, including himself, for purely artistic purposes as if they were so many syllables; when he can therefore endow them with such independent life that they can work out their history—however preordained by him—in accordance with their own natures and, as far as they are concerned, by their own free will.[17] At this stage, says Stephen in the *Portrait,* "the personality of the artist . . . refines itself out of existence." Thus life is purified and reprojected from an imagination as free as a mathematician's, and "the mystery of esthetic like that of material creation is accomplished." The author, like God, is completely detached, "invisible, refined out of existence, indifferent" (252). The final clause, however, "paring his fingernails," is a giveaway (doubtless intentional) of both Stephen and Joyce. A person who is really indifferent has no need for such a self-conscious pantomime of indifference. That is a fair description of *Finnegans Wake.*

In the *Portrait* Stephen does not quite claim to be God; he calls himself rather "the priest of the eternal imagination" (260); on the beach, after having decided not to join the Jesuits, he discovers the one God he can serve, art: the art of using language to express the meaning of life—and to create meaning—in works whose beauty is a matter of their perfect efficacy (190–201). The principle is illustrated in the Telemachus and Eumaeus episodes of *Ulysses.* When Stephen composes the phrase, "white breast of the dim sea," what interests and pleases him is not so much the sea as the phrase itself and his own activity as poet: "The twining stresses, two by two. A hand plucking the harpstrings merging their twining chords. Wavewhite wedded words shimmering on the dim tide" (11). This is the work of a linguistic genius who, like Augustine, thinks of poetry chiefly in terms of its musical qualities.

Joyce, however, recognizes the limitations of that view. When

Bloom, passing a group of Italians, is charmed by the sound of their speech—"it is so melodious and full"—Stephen wearily informs him that they are "haggling over money" (606). Yet Bloom is not deluded until he devalues his own experience by saying, "It may be only the southern glamour that surrounds it." His naïve first impression was right: animated speech has a beauty of its own, regardless of content or vocabulary, and certainly *"Putanna madonna, che ci dia i quattrini!"* (605), for all its obscene irreverence, is as musical as "white breast of the dim sea." Yet Stephen is right too, for the content is certainly offensive and if we perceive it we cannot honestly ignore it. Joyce, however, being above Stephen, Bloom and the quarreling Italians, uses the ludicrous unlovely incident to create a complex beauty, that artistic beauty which Stephen calls in the *Portrait* the radiance of truth (243, 250)—the revelation of the inner and outer relations of things and thus of their meaning. This does not shine from the Italians' speech or from anything that Bloom or Stephen says about it; there is little natural beauty in any one of these elements, but Joyce creates artistic beauty from them by showing us the truth of which they are an epiphany and by making us admire the skill with which he shows it. Bloom's pitifully dull remark about Southern glamour, for example, is so justly recorded that the contemplation of the recording gives us an intellectual pleasure of the aesthetic kind. Thus, just as God accomplishes His good work through man's bad works, so the priest of the imagination creates beauty from ugly materials— or rather, as Stephen would say, expresses the beauty he can see in their relations. There is thus an essentially romantic attitude behind all Joyce's work, however unromantic the details may seem, and an essentially Augustinian acceptance of things as they are. Augustine came to acceptance through religion, Joyce through art. One is perhaps as evil as the other.

The artist's task, however, is more difficult, for he must at all times be clearheaded about his work, and the priestly imagination is liable to a peculiarly seductive kind of doublethink. The priest is a vicar, a vicarious God, so that even though he denies that he is God he can hardly help acting as if he were. However

long the chain of command may be, still the Pope is God's vicar
and the village priest acts for him; the village priest, no less than
the Pope, can hardly permit himself to be gainsaid, and is therefore liable to regard all who disagree with him in anything as
enemies of God. Joyce's self-confidence seems to have been of this
kind. He tended to regard those who disagreed with him as enemies of art. He was always a man of faith; as an adult he lived
by the truth of art as intensely as he had formerly lived by the
truth of the Catholic religion. In the *Portrait* Stephen deplores
a girl's preferring the false priest of Catholicism, who merely
goes through the motions of communion with the divine, to himself, in whom divinity lives although as yet there are no outward
signs of it (259–260). What he deplores in her is lack of faith,
lack of that spiritual vision which would have enabled her to
make a better choice. He frankly regards himself as one of the
elect of his race, in betraying whom the mocker Moynihan (a
forerunner of Buck Mulligan) betrays the whole race (226). In
Ulysses he deplores the old milkwoman's preferring Mulligan to
himself (16), and Joyce implies that the barmaids at the Ormond
are equally blind in preferring the mocker Boylan, in whom
there is no truth, to the good Bloom, who in his fallen condition is yet also a man of faith (256, 262). In *Finnegans Wake*
Shem "lifts the lifewand and the dumb speak" (195), but the
Leapyear Girls have no use for him; they flock around Shaun,
though—or because—"he points the deathbone and the quick
are still" (193, 595). This is one of the major themes of Joyce's
work as a whole: the tendency of "ordinary people," as Stephen
Hero says, to commit "moral suicide" (200–201) or to reveal the
fact that they are already dead by choosing Barabbas instead of
God. "No honourable and sincere man," says Stephen to the
nationalists in the *Portrait*, "has given up to you his life and
his youth and his affections . . . but you sold him to the enemy
or failed him in need or reviled him and left him for another.
And you invite me to be one of you. I'd see you damned first"
(237–238). He himself does not fear to be "spurned for another"
(292). He thus explicitly rejects not the role of savior but the role
of one who kills the savior. His attitude is close to that of God

in the *Enchiridion,* who willingly sees the majority of men damned because it is their nature to be damned.[18]

But God is the savior too—of those who by His own decree have natures capable of being saved. Stephen likewise, as artist, hopes to save from spiritual death those who are capable of being quickened by his art: "How could he hit their conscience or how cast his shadow over the imaginations of their daughters, before their squires begat upon them, that they might breed a race less ignoble than their own?" (280). The answer Joyce proposed can be found in his youthful criticism and in all his works: the art itself must create its audience—must create those who can respond to it and be saved. Not the majority, of course, who have no desire to rise any higher than they must, but the elect, who by their aspiration cut themselves off from the majority.

The artist who ministers to and in part creates aspiration is not quite God, but his activity is godlike. He makes the most difficult of all human choices. He risks cutting himself off from all human understanding, for a purpose which may very well turn out to be of no consequence after all. Joyce made that hard decision. So great was his faith in art, he was willing to risk damnation for it. In the *Portrait* Stephen tells Cranly, "I am not afraid to make a mistake, even a great mistake, a lifelong mistake and perhaps as long as eternity too." To Cranly's question if he would be willing to stand "quite alone . . . separate from all others" and "to have not even one friend," he replies, "I will take the risk" (292). Joyce suffered intensely from his isolation, but contrived to create beauty from it: the picture of Shem in *Finnegans Wake* is a nightmare of loneliness (169–187), but the author looks down and describes it with godlike levity and joy. He is never completely detached, because he can never quite forget that he is being detached, and because after all he is not without human passion. His own voice can be heard in Anna Livia's cry, "A hundred cares, a tithe of troubles and is there one who understands me?" (627); he knows that in eternity not only his own work but all life, all variety, all joy and all creation will be drowned in the conformity of death and total darkness; nevertheless he

will continue to lift the lifewand that the dumb may sing the song of the universe

> Till tree from tree, tree among trees, tree over tree become stone to stone, stone between stones, stone under stone for ever (259).

That is perhaps as near to the purely intellectual joy of **God** as man can come.

Notes

CHAPTER I

1. J.-P. Migne, *Patrologia Latina*, CXXII, 509A, 511B, 513B-C.
2. This *terminus a quo* is rather arbitrary. I ignore Porphyry and Boethius, who first stated the problem, because they were not involved in the controversy over it; and of course the controversy was implicit in Plato.
3. Migne, *P.L.*, CL, 421C-D: "Sed, sicut dicit Andreas apostolus, cum vere in terris carnes ejus sint comestae et vere sanguis ejus sit bibitus, ipse tamen usque in tempora restitutionis omnium in coelestibus ad dexteram Patris integer perseverat et vivus. Si quaeris modum quo id fieri possit, breviter ad praesens respondeo: Mysterium fidei credi salubriter potest, vestigari utiliter non potest."
4. *Ibid.*, CLVIII, 262A: "Si in Deo tres personae sunt una tantum res; ut non sunt tres res unaquaeque per se separatim, sicut tres angeli, aut tres animae; ita tamen ut potentia et voluntate omnino sint idem: ergo Pater et Spiritus sanctus cum Filio est incarnatus."
5. *Ibid.*, 265B-C: "Qui enim nondum intelligit quomodo plures homines in species sint unus homo; qualiter in illa secretissima et altissima natura comprehendet quomodo plures personae, quarum singula quaeque est perfectus Deus, sint unus Deus? . . . Haec dixi, ne quis antequam sit idoneus, altissimas de fidei quaestiones praesumat discutere." ["If one cannot understand the way in which several men can be in species one mankind, how can he comprehend in its highest and most hidden nature the way in which several Persons, each of whom singly is the perfect God, can be one God? . . . I said that one who is not able should not presume to discuss the highest questions of faith."]
6. *Ibid.*, 263C: "Si potest intelligere, Deo gratias agat; si non potest, non immittat cornua ad ventilandum, sed submittat caput ad venerandum." ["If he can understand, let him thank God; if he cannot, let him not toss his horns in the air but bow his head in reverence."]
7. Johann Eduard Erdmann, *A History of Philosophy*, trans. by Williston S. Hough (London, 1890–1892), I, 312.

8. Hope Emily Allen, *Writings Ascribed to Richard Rolle, . . .* (New York, 1927), pp. 316, 347.

9. See *Yorkshire Writers: Richard Rolle of Hampole and His Followers,* ed. by C. Horstman[n] (London, 1896), II, xxx: "Mundi amatores scire possunt verba vel carmina nostrarum cantionum, non autem cantica nostrorum carminium. . . . Ipsi insipidi divina sapientia non imbuti sed scientia acquisita inflati, male de seipsis senciunt et Deum adhuc cum amore tenere nesciunt. . . . Ego Ricardus solitarius heremita dictus hoc melius cognovi quia expertus sum; or: hoc quod novi, assero." ["Lovers of the world can understand the words or verses of our song, but not the song of our verses. . . . These savorless people, not imbued with divine wisdom but puffed up with acquired knowledge, wickedly follow their own perceptions and do not know how to cling to God with love. . . . I, Richard, the so-called solitary hermit, know better, for I have had the experience; what I know, therefore, I assert."]

10. Migne, *P.L.,* CXCIX, 664B-D.

11. *Ibid.,* 640B-D.

12. *Ibid.,* 866B-C, 942A-C.

13. For Bacon's appreciation of the mathematical and experimental methods, see *The Opus Majus of Roger Bacon,* trans. by Robert Bell Burke (Philadelphia, 1928), I, 123–127; II, 583–584.

14. See Dorothy E. Sharp, *Franciscan Philosophy at Oxford in the Thirteenth Century* (Oxford, 1930), p. 117.

15. *Ibid.,* pp. 336–341. The journalist Anne Fremantle, in *The Age of Belief* (New York: New American Library, 1955), p. 182, has unfortunately got it backwards.

16. *B. Ioannis Duns Scoti . . . Commentaria Oxoniensia,* ed. by Marianus Fernandez Garcia (Quaracchi, 1914), II, 658–661. On God as uncaused and uncausable first cause, see *The De Primo Principio of John Duns Scotus,* ed. and trans. by Evan Roche (St. Bonaventure, N.Y., 1949), pp. 67, 89, 143.

17. *B. Ioannis Duns Scoti . . . Commentaria Oxoniensia,* II, 728–733.

18. See Erigena, *De Divina Praedestinatione* (Migne, *P.L.,* CXXII, 378B-C); *De Divisione Naturae* (Migne, *P.L.,* CXXII, 810–829). For Augustine's view, see Chapter VIII of this book. Since Augustine's God is an artist, the good He achieves is aesthetic rather than moral, cosmic rather than human. This is one reason, I believe, that the schoolmen turned away from Augustine to Aristotle, thus taking a step in the direction of nominalism.

19. *Summa Theologica,* I, Q. 85, Art. 3, Reply Obj. 4.

20. *B. Ioannis Duns Scoti* . . . *Commentaria Oxoniensia,* II, 237–238, 241–242; *De Primo Principio,* pp. 21–23.
21. See Allan Bernard Wolter, *The Transcendentals and Their Function in the Metaphysics of Duns Scotus* (Washington, 1946), pp. 15–16, 27–29.
22. *B. Ioannis Duns Scoti* . . . *Commentaria Oxoniensia,* II, 269–270, §289.
23. Sharp, pp. 282–283.
24. Thomas Netter, *Fasciculi Zizaniorum* . . . , ed. by Walter W. Shirley (London: Rolls Series, No. 5, 1858), p. xlix.
25. See Herbert B. Workman, *John Wyclif: A Study of the English Medieval Church* (Oxford, 1926), I, 111.
26. Robert Guelluy, *Philosophie et théologie chez Guillaume d'Ockham* (Louvain, 1947), pp. 13, 376; Etienne Gilson, *La Philosophie au Moyen Age* (3d ed.; Paris, 1947), p. 655.
27. Guelluy, pp. 17–19; Gilson, p. 639.
28. Léon Baudry, "Le Philosophe et le politique dans Guillaume d'Ockham," *Archives d'histoire doctrinale et littéraire du Moyen Age,* XII (1939), 215–220.
29. Stephen Chak Tornay, *Ockham: Studies and Selections* (La Salle, Ill., 1938), pp. 119, 126–128.
30. *Ibid.,* pp. 132, 139–140, 144. Cf. Ockham's *Summa Logicae,* Part I, ed. by Philotheus Boehner (St. Bonaventure, N.Y., 1951), pp. 59–65.
31. Baudry, pp. 213–214.
32. *Ibid.,* pp. 213–217, 221.
33. *The De Sacramento Altaris of William of Ockham,* trans. by T. Bruce Birch (Burlington, Iowa, 1930), p. xxiii.
34. Léon Baudry, "A propos de Guillaume d'Ockham et de Wiclef," *Archives d'histoire doctrinale et littéraire du Moyen Age,* XII (1939), 251.
35. Tornay, pp. 173, 179, 189, 194–195.
36. Joseph H. Dahmus, *The Prosecution of John Wyclif* (New Haven, Conn., 1952), p. 81.
37. Workman, I, 136ff.; II, 12, 33.
38. *De Sacramento Altaris,* pp. 112–113, 114
39. *Fasciculi Zizaniorum,* pp. 105–106.
40. *Ibid.,* pp. 115–132.
41. *Chronicon Angliae* . . . *Auctore Monacho Quodam Sancti Albani,* ed. by Edward M. Thompson (London: Rolls Series, No. 64, 1874), p. 395: "Inter alia dicunt et asserunt quod Eukaristia in altari post sacramentum non est verum corpus Christi, sed ejus figura."

42. On the difference between Wyclif and the Lollards, see K. B. McFarlane, *John Wyclif and the Beginnings of English Non-Conformity* (New York, 1953), pp. 99–102; Ezra K. Maxfield, "Chaucer and Religious Reform," *PMLA*, XXXIX (1924), 64–74.

43. *The English Works of Wyclif Hitherto Unprinted*, ed. by F. D. Matthew (EETS No. 74), pp. 341–342, 345.

CHAPTER II

1. *The City of God*, XI, 9, trans. by Marcus Dods (New York: Modern Library, 1950), p. 354.

2. *Confessions*, VII, 12, trans. by E. B. Pusey (London: Everyman, 1907), p. 135.

3. *Dialogue on Truth*, VII, ed. by Richard McKeon, *Selections from Medieval Philosophers* (New York, 1929), I, 164.

4. Cf. John of Salisbury, *Policraticus*, IV, 1 (J.-P. Migne, *Patrologia Latina*, CXCIX, 514A): "Neque enim potentis est, cum vult saevire in subditos, sed divinae dispensationis, pro beneplacito sua punire, vel exercere subjectos." ["When he [the prince] wills to be cruel to his subjects, it is not by his own authority but by the dispensation of God, who is pleased to punish or test them."]

5. Herbert Gorman, *James Joyce* (New York, 1948), p. 73.

6. *De Divisione Naturae*, V, 27–28 (Migne, *P.L.*, CXXII, 928D–938B). Cf. Augustine, *The City of God*, XI, 17, p. 361; XIX, 13, p. 691.

7. Euripides, *Iphigenia in Tauris*, trans. by Witter Bynner (New York, 1925), p. 52.

8. *The City of God*, XI, 18, p. 361.

9. *De Musica*, VI, xvii, 56 (Migne, *P.L.*, XXXII, 1191 [B]): "Deus autem summe bonus, et summe justus, nulli invidet pulchritudini, quae sive damnatione animae, sive regressione, sive permansione fabricatur." Cf. *De Libero Arbitrio*, III, xiii, 36 (Migne, *P.L.*, XXXII, 1289[B]–1290[A]).

10. Flaubert, *Correspondance* (Paris, 1926–1933), III, 61–62; IV, 164; V, 227–228; VII, 280. That Stephen's aesthetic ideas were Joyce's own is indicated by the excerpts from Joyce's notebooks quoted in Herbert Gorman's biography, pp. 95–99, 133–135.

11. Augustine, *The City of God*, XI, 17–18, pp. 361–362. Cf. Paul Valéry,

Mon Faust (Paris, 1946), p. 7: "Mais rien ne démontre plus sûrement la puissance d'un créateur que l'infidélité ou l'insoumission de sa créature. Plus il l'a faite vivante, plus il l'a faite libre. Même sa rébellion exalte son auteur: Dieu le sait."

12. *Confessions,* X, 41, p. 229. This division did not originate with Augustine. He himself refers us to I John 1:16.
13. *Confessions,* X, 43–47, pp. 231–233. Cf. Aristotle, *Nicomachean Ethics,* X, iii, 6.
14. *Ayenbite of Inwyt,* ed. by Richard Morris (London: EETS No. 23, 1866), pp. 50, 54. Cf. quotation from Joyce's notebook, Gorman, p. 136: "Church calls it a low vice . . . to make a God of the belly."
15. Migne, *P.L.,* CXIX, 1052C: "Fuge itaque principatum nequitur usurpatum."
16. *De Musica,* VI, xi, 30; *De Libero Arbitrio,* II, xix, 53; III, ix, 26; III, xi, 32 (Migne, *P.L.,* XXXII, 1179[D]–1180[B]; 1269[A-B]; 1283[D]–1284[B]; 1287[A–B]).
17. *Confessions,* X, 41, p. 229. Cf. the *Portrait,* p. 111.
18. *Ayenbite,* p. 158.
19. *Ibid.,* pp. 46–47, 202. Cf. Chaucer, *The Persones Tale,* §20.
20. *Confessions,* X, 48, p. 234.
21. *Ayenbite,* p. 91.
22. *Ibid.,* p. 177.
23. *Confessions,* X, 49, pp. 234–235.
24. *Ayenbite,* p. 177.
25. *Ibid.,* pp. 57–70, 254–258.
26. *Confessions,* X, 51–52, pp. 236–237.
27. *Ayenbite,* pp. 46, 177.
28. *Confessions,* X, 54, pp. 238–239.
29. Cf., for example, M.-D. Chenu, "Grammaire et théologie aux XIIe et XIIIe siècles," *Archives d'histoire doctrinale et littéraire du Moyen Age,* 1935, X, 5–31; Etienne Gilson, *Jean Duns Scot, Introduction à ses positions fondamentales* (Paris, 1952), p. 602. For some direct quotations, cf. Migne, *P.L.,* II, 19A–21A; LXXVII, 1171C–1172A; CXLV, 306C, 307D; CL, 421D; CXCVI, 34C. On the Protestant side, cf. Richard Foster Jones, "The Attack on Pulpit Eloquence in the Restoration," in *The Seventeenth Century* (Stanford, 1951).
30. *Ayenbite,* pp. 81–82.
31. *Ibid.,* pp. 50–51. Cf. Chaucer, *The Persones Tale,* §72.
32. Migne, *P.L.,* XXXII, 1023[A]: "Porro quod sic agitur, et exspecta-tione opus ut peragi, et memoria ut comprehendi queat quantum

potest. Et exspectatio futurarum rerum est, praeteritarum vero memoria. At intentio ad agendum praesentis est temporis, per quod futurum in praeteritum transit."

33. Aristotle, *Physics*, IV, xi, trans. by Philip H. Wicksteed and Francis M. Cornford (London: Loeb Classics, 1929), I, 389.

CHAPTER III

1. HCE sees his phallic skyscraper "erigenating from next to nothing." Next to zero comes the One, the Neo-Platonic God, which in Its transcendence of attributes is next to nothing.

2. Cf., for example, W. Y. Tindall, "James Joyce and the Hermetic Tradition," *JHI*, XV, 1 (January, 1954), 23–39. Joyce's use of similar ideas in Hindu myth and the Cabala is well known.

3. *Republic*, III, 399. Milton, in the *Areopagitica*, suggests that the *Republic* flowed from "the *genial* cups of an *Academick* night-sitting."

4. *De Divina Praedestinatione*, V, 8 (J.-P. Migne, *Patrologia Latina*, CXXII, 378B-C): "Si Deus in homine talem voluntatem condidisset, quae non omnimodo movere se posset, sive recte, sive perverse, non omnimodo libera esset, sed esset ex parte libera, ex parte non libera; libera quidem juste, non autem injuste vivere. Si ergo esset aliqua ex parte necessitas, non esset perfecto libertas." ["If God had given man a will that could not move in all ways, whether rightly or perversely, it would not be entirely free, but partly free and partly not free; free to live justly, but not unjustly. Thus, if it were in any way subject to necessity, its liberty would not be perfect."] But God had no board of trustees.

5. *De Divisione Naturae*, IV, 15 (Migne, *P.L.*, CXXII, 811C-D): "Prius ergo descendebat de paradiso, suae voluntatis irrationabili motu impulsus, et . . . in defectum instabilitatemque rerum temporalium [praecipitabatur]; et cadendo vulneratus est, omnibusque naturalibus bonis, in quibus conditus erat, spoliatus. Ubi datur intelligi, quod homo in se ipso lapsus est, quam diabolo tentaretur; nec hoc solum, verum etiam, quod non in paradiso, sed descendente eo, propriaque voluntate a paradisi felicitate, . . . hoc est visionis pacis intelligitur, deserente, et . . . in hunc mundum labente a diabolo sauciatus sit, et beatitudine spoliatus. Non enim credibile est, eundem hominem et

in contemplatione aeternae pacis stetisse, et suadente femina serpentis veneno corrupta corruisse, aut ipsum serpentem, diabolum dico, jam de paradiso, dignitate videlicet angelicae naturae, lapsum, in homine adhuc non peccante, neque celsitudine divinae imaginis corruente praevaluisse." ["He therefore fell from Paradise previously [to being tempted], impelled by the irrational motion of his will, and was hurled headlong into the imperfection and instability of temporal things; by that fall he was damaged, and lost all the good qualities with which he was made. By which we are given to understand that man fell by himself rather than by the Devil's temptation; and moreover it was not in Paradise but while descending from it, while deserting by his own free will the felicity of Paradise—that is to say, the vision of peace—and while falling into this world that he was smitten by the Devil and robbed of blessedness. Nor indeed is it credible that man could both remain in contemplation of the eternal peace and be persuaded to fall from it by woman (corrupted by the serpent's venom), or that the serpent himself, I mean the Devil, now fallen from Paradise—that is, from the dignity of the angelic nature—could prevail on man if man had not already sinned and declined from the loftiness of the divine image."] On the allegorical nature of the Scriptures, cf. 509A. For the orthodox view, cf. Augustine, *The City of God,* XIII, 21.

6. Migne, *P.L.,* CXXII, 817D, 835C–836B: "Ac per hoc in geminum sexum scissus est, in masculum videlicet et feminam: quae discissio non ex natura, sed ex vitio causam accepit. . . . Siquidem sopor ille et causa peccati et post peccatum immissus. . . . Ubi notandum, quod, postquam obdormivit Adam, conditionem mulieris introduxit Scriptura, ut per hoc insinuaret, quod, si humana natura simplicem sinceramque integritatem suae constitutionis, qua ad imaginem Dei facta est, irrationabili motu liberae voluntatis non desereret, sed semper in contemplatione veritatis incommutabiliter permaneret, omnino scissuram suam in duplicem sexum ad similitudinem irrationabilium animalium non pateretur, sed eo modo, quo angelicus numerus sine ullo sexu multiplicatus est, multiplicaretur."

7. *Ibid.,* 836C: "In primo siquidem Adam scissa est natura in masculum et feminam, in secundo adunata est. In Christo enim Jesu non est masculus neque femina. In primo universa natura de felicitate paradisi est expulsa, in secundo in eandem felicitatem est revocata et restituta."

8. *Ibid.,* 836D–837C.

9. For the orthodox view, cf. Augustine, *The City of God*, XXII, 17; Hugh of St. Victor, *On the Sacraments of the Christian Faith*, I, 8.

10. Mrs. Adaline Glasheen informs me that sucking the ruler's breast was a symbol of fealty in ancient Ireland.

CHAPTER IV

1. *Confessions*, IV, 1, trans. by E. B. Pusey (London: Everyman, 1907), p. 50. The word Pusey translates "workhouse" is *officina*, workshop.

2. A "true spell" is a *Treuspiel* or confidence game, to which Cain will not rise—that is, for which he will not fall. Connacht was the first center of Irish nationalism; but its king, Rory O'Conor, was the first to legalize English rule, and various treacheries were subsequently perpetrated there. As the seat of Tara, it may also be construed as Paradise. Cf. Tom Ireland, *Ireland Past and Present* (New York, 1922), pp. 44, 74, 131, 159. Mrs. Adaline Glasheen tells me there is also an allusion here to Oliver Cromwell's remark, "The Irish can go to Hell or Connacht," Connacht being no Paradise but a particularly barren and undesirable place. Cromwell, who fought for liberty in England but suppressed it in Ireland, illustrates Joyce's view of the ambivalence of human tendencies.

3. J.-P. Migne, *Patrologia Latina*, CLVIII, 726C, 793A-B: "Heu! de quam sublimi cecidisti, in quam profundum corruisti! Vae! quam benignum contempsisti, quam maligno te junxisti! Quid fecisti, O mentis amentia, amens spurcitia, spurca nequitia, quid fecisti? . . . Deus meus, quo abii? quo fugi? quo evasi? Ejectus a facie tua sicut Cain, habitavi in terra vagus et profugus, et quicunque invenerit me, occidet me."

4. *Ibid.*, 263C: "Si potest intelligere, Deo gratias agat; si non potest, non immittat cornua ad ventilandum, sed submittat caput ad venerandum."

5. *Stephen Hero* (New York, 1955), p. 73.

6. *Ibid.*, p. 57. Cf. the *Portrait*, Chs. III–IV.

7. Caseous is here identified with Jesus.

8. Ambrose, *De Cain et Abel* (Migne, *P.L.*, XIV, 318A-B): "Haec figura Synagogae et Ecclesiae in his duobus fratribus ante praecessit Cain et Abel. Per Cain parricidalis populus intelligitur Judaeorum. . . . Per Abel autem intelligitur Christianus adhaerens Deo." ["The Syna-

gogue and the Church were prefigured in these two brothers, Cain and Abel. By the parricidal Cain is to be understood the nation of the Jews. . . . By Abel, on the other hand, is to be understood the Christian adhering to God."] This idea is repeated by every author I have looked into.

9. Isidore, Bishop of Seville, *Allegoriae Quaedam Sacrae Scripturae* (Migne, *P.L.*, LXXXIII, 99A): "Abel, pastor ovium, Christi tenuit typum, qui est verus, et bonus pastor." ["Abel, a shepherd of sheep, constituted the type of Christ, who is the true and good shepherd."]

10. Saint Cyprian of Carthage, *De Oratione Dominica* (Migne, *P.L.*, IV, 553B–554A): "Abel pacificus et justus . . . qui et justitiam Domini habuerat et pacem." ["The peaceful and just Abel, . . . who had the justice and peace of the Lord."] Saint Paschasius Radbertus, *Expositio in Matthaeum*, IX, 20 (Migne, *P.L.*, CXX, 674D): ". . . ab Abel justo usque ad illum ultimum electum qui in fine mundi venturus est colligitur." [". . . from the just Abel to the last of those elect who at the end of the world will come to be gathered together."] Cf. Matthew 23:35.

11. Saint Maxim, *Homilia LV* (Migne, *P.L.*, LVII, 355C): "Abel justus . . . et innocens . . ." ["Abel, just . . . and innocent . . ."]

12. Saint Cyprian, *De Bono Patientiae* (Migne, *P.L.*, IV, 652C): "Abel, adversus fratrem fratricidam non resistit nec reluctatur, sed humilis et mitis patienter occiditur." ["Abel neither resisted nor fought his fratricidal brother, but, humble and meek, patiently suffered death."]

13. Saint Cyprian, *Epistola LVI* (Migne, *P.L.*, IV, 363A-B): "Imitemur, fratres dilectissimi, Abel justum, qui initiavit martyria dum propter justitiam primus occiditur." ["Let us imitate, dearest brothers, the just Abel, who initiated the practice of martyrdom, being the first to be killed because of his justice."] Saint Paulinus of Nola, *Epistola XXXIII* (Migne, *P.L.*, LXI, 359A): "Ab initio saeculorum Christus in omnibus suis patitur. Ipse est initium et finis, qui . . . in Abel occisus a fratre, . . . et multis ac variis beatorum martyrum crucibus frequenter occisus." ["From the earliest ages Christ was made manifest in all who are His. He is the first and the last, who . . . in Abel, killed by his brother, . . . and in many and various martyrs was often killed on the cross."]

14. Saint Maxim, *Homilia LV* (Migne, *P.L.*, LVII, 355B-C): "Ab initio saeculi et praedicta sunt oraculis, et praefigurata mysteriis. . . . Itaque in Domini nostra persona, . . . ex hujus sacro latere ac salutari vulnere Ecclesia omnium fidelium parens reparanda monstratur. In ejus typo Abel justus occiditur." ["From the beginning of the world

the prophecies were foreshadowed and the mysteries were prefigured. . . . Likewise in the person of our Lord, . . . from whose sacred body and saving wounds the church, parent of all the faithful, is shown to rise. As a type of Him the just Abel was killed."]

15. Saint Philastrius, *Liber de Haeresibus*, CXXXI (Migne, *P.L.*, XII, 1261A): "Sunt haeretici contraria sentientes libro Geneseos, que Dominus dixerit ad Cain: *Peccasti, quiesce.*" ["It is the heretics against whom the Lord spoke the words in the book of Genesis against Cain: 'Thou hast sinned; hold thy peace.'" (This is Genesis 4:7 in the Septuagint—ἥμαρτες; ἡσύχασον—which the Latin fathers generally followed. The first clause is mistranslated; it is actually a question: "Hast thou not sinned?")] Cf. Ambrose, *De Incarnationis Dominicae Sacramento*, II (Migne, *P.L.*, XVI, 821A): "Adversus omnes igitur haereses ista sententia est." ["Therefore that sentence is pronounced against all heretics."] He specifies the Arians, Sabellians, Manichaeans, Valentinians, and Donatists.

16. *The City of God*, XV, 1, trans. by Marcus Dods (New York: Modern Library, 1950), pp. 478–479.

17. *De Cain et Abel*, I, 4 (Migne, *P.L.*, XIV, 317B-C): "Duae itaque sectae sunt sub duorum fratrum nomine compugnantes invicem, et contrariae sibi. Ubi quae totum menti suae deputat tamquam principali, et quasi quidam cogitationis, et sensus, et motus omnis auctori; hoc est, quae omnes inventiones humano ascribit ingenio. Altera quae tamquam operatori et creatori omnium Deo defert, et ejus tamquam parentis atque rectoris subdit omnia gubernaculo. Illa prior, Cain significatur; haec posterior, Abel dicitur. Has duas sectas una anima parturit; et ideo germanae habentur, quod uno fundantur utero: sed contrariae sunt; quia oportet eas cum quodam animae partu editae fuerint, dividi ac separari. Compugnantibus enim hospitium unum perpetuo esse non potest."

18. *The City of God*, XV, 5, pp. 482–483.

19. *Allegoriae Quaedam Sacrae Scripturae* (Migne, *P.L.*, LXXXIII, 99A): "Enoch, filius Cain, in cujus nomine pater condidit civitatem, significat impios in hac tantum vita esse fundatos."

20. *De Trinitate et Operibus Ejus* (Migne, *P.L.*, CLXVII, 336B): "Notandum tandem quod prima terrenarum civitatum causa homicidium sit. Nam quia Cain fratrem suum occiderat, et ob hoc omnibus odiosus, vagusque et profugus super terram erat, idcirco civitatem qua tutaretur aedificavit, egressus, id est profectus a facie Domini, nec habens sortem in civitate ejus coelesti."

21. Cf. *Finnegans Wake*, p. 94: "framm Sin fromm Son, acity arose."

22. Tertullian, *De Patientia,* V (Migne, *P.L.,* I, 1258A): "Quod enim ipsum Adam et Evam morti immiserat, docuit et filium ab homicido incipere. Frustra istud impatientiae adscripserim, si Cain ille primus homicida, et primus fratricida, oblationes suas a Domino recusatas aequanimiter nec impatienter tulit." ["That very thing [impatience] that had plunged Adam and Eve into death also taught their son to begin with homicide. It would be idle to ascribe this to impatience if Cain, that first homicide and first fratricide, had borne equably and not impatiently the Lord's refusal of his oblations."]

23. Cf. Michel Carrouges, *La Mystique du surhomme* (Paris, 1948), pp. 17, 326–327.

24. Alcuin, *Commentaria in S. Joannis Evangelium* (Migne, *P.L.,* C, 768B): "In primum aetate saeculi, Abel justum frater invidens occidit." ["In the first age of the world, the just Abel was killed by his envious brother."] Cf. Augustine, *loc. cit.*

25. Ambrose, *De Cain et Abel,* I, 4 (Migne, *P.L.,* XIV, 353B–355A): "Omnia docet Deus. Primum ne pecces, ut in Adam monuit: secundo, si pecces, quiescas, ut in Cain doceris. . . . Confessio enim poenarum compendium est. . . . Est quaedam in peccatis verecundia, et poenitentiae portio crimen fateri, nec derivare culpam, sed recognoscere. Mitigat judicem pudor reorum, excitat autem pertinacia denegantium." ["God teaches all things. First, do not sin, as he warned us in Adam; second, if you sin, hold your peace, as he taught us in Cain. . . . Confession indeed mitigates punishments. . . . There is a certain shamefulness in sin, and the part of penitence is to acknowledge the reproach—not to evade the guilt, but to recognize it. Shame for our deeds mitigates the sentence, pertinacity in denying them increases it."]

26. There is a precedent for portraying Justice as a prig, in Spenser's Artegall.

27. The "artthoudux," who questions the leader's leadership, is unorthodox; the "heterotropic," who is oriented toward others, is a conformist. He anticipates David Riesman's "other-directed" personality!

28. Shaun unwittingly reveals himself. "Fiend" is of course a Freudian slip for "friend." "With" has its original sense of "at" or "against." "Game loser" means not only "good loser" but "one who loses games." (Recall the laughter of the Ondt.) "Disk," in this context, means "hat"; but the word is cognate with "dish" and means among other things the surface containing the oral cavity in several low forms of life.

29. W. Y. Tindall, *James Joyce* (New York, 1950), p. 80.

30. I owe the whole account of Minthē, including this quotation, to the Pauly *Real-Encyclopädie der Classischen Altertumswissenschaft.*
31. For this and the preceding quotation, cf. Arthur Bernard Cook, *Zeus: A Study in Ancient Religion* (Cambridge, England, 1914–1925–1940), II, 1163–1167. It is worth noting that this volume, published in 1925, bears the subtitle "God of the Dark Sky (Thunder and Lightning)."
32. Cf. *Nicomachean Ethics,* III, 11: "Such insensibility is not human."
33. *Ireland Past and Present,* pp. 130–156.
34. *The Trial of Jeanne d'Arc,* trans. by W. P. Barrett (New York, 1932), pp. 55, 154. Since Joyce's language here suggests French, "all Saint" suggests Toussaint, another fighter for national independence who was betrayed. Napoleon, the betrayer, was a transformation of Saint Joan: another example of ambivalence.
35. James G. Frazer, *The Golden Bough* (London, 1913–1915), II, 92–96. Cf. my article, "The Unity of the Revesby Sword Play," *PQ,* XXXIII, 1 (January, 1954), 83, n. 15.

CHAPTER V

1. Joseph Campbell and Henry Morton Robinson, *A Skeleton Key to Finnegans Wake* (New York, 1944), p. 24.
2. Cf. Augustine, *The City of God,* XI, 17–18, trans. by Marcus Dods (New York: Modern Library, 1950), p. 361.
3. This was a prevalent notion in the Middle Ages; cf. the *Poema Morale* and Aelfric's life of Saint Eugenia.
4. I follow the interpretation of Thomas Mann, *Joseph and His Brothers* (New York, 1934), pp. 213–232.
5. Herbert Gorman, *James Joyce* (New York, 1948), p. 93.
6. Giordano Bruno described himself as "In tristitia hilaris, hilaritate tristis." Cf. J. Lewis McIntyre, *Giordano Bruno* (London, 1903), p. 19. The "prankquean" seems to be a blend of the Princess Graine Ni Maille, the nurse who kidnaped Jonathan Swift, and the goddess Fortuna, who, like rain, visits playboys and saints indiscriminately.
7. Gorman, p. 73.
8. Ambrose, *De Jacob et Vita Beata,* II, 3 (J.-P. Migne, *Patrologia Latina,* XIV, 619B-C): "Servit omnis qui auctoritatem purae non habet

conscientiae: servit quicumque vel metu frangitur, vel delectatione irretitur, vel cupiditatibus ducitur, vel indignatione exasperatur, vel moerore dejicitur. Servilis enim est omnis passio; quoniam qui facit peccatum, servus est peccati, et quod pejus est, multorum servus est: qui subjectus est vitiis, multis se dominis addixit, ut servitio ei exire vix liceat. At vero ille qui voluntatis suae arbiter est, judex consilii, interpres arbitrii, qui coercet corporeae appetentiam passionis, qui eaquae agit, bene agit, bene autem agens recte agit, et qui recte agit, inculpate et irreprehensibiliter agit, habens suorum actuum potestatem; is profecto liber est." Cf. Plato, *Republic*, I, 329.

9. Augustine, *Sermo IV, De Jacob et Esau*, III (Migne, *P.L.*, XXXVIII, 34 [B-C]): "Esau carnales, Jacob spirtuales figurat."

10. Augustine, *Sermones Supposititios*, X, "De Conceptu Rebeccae" Migne, *P.L.*, XXXVIII, 1759[D]–1760[A]): "De uno ergo semine Isaac, Esau nascitur et Jacob: sicut de uno Baptismo Domini Salvatoris et de uno Ecclesiae utero procreatur populus Christianus: qui tamen pro morum diversitate, sicut Esau et Jacob, in duas partes dividitur; cum ex fructibus operum una pars cogniscitur carnalis, alia spiritualis. Ideo autem dixit, *Major serviet minori*, quia semper major est numerus malorum quam bonorum. Et sicut illi duo parvuli in utero Rebeccae; ita et isti duo populi in ventre Ecclesiae usque in diem judicii colliduntur; dum, sicut jam supra diximus, humilibus adversantur superbi, dum castos adulteri persequuntur, dum, quorum infinitus est numerus, ebriosi sobrios insectantur, dum benignos invidi aemulantur, dum eleemosynarios raptores, dum pacificos exstinguere cupiunt iracundi, dum eos qui coelestia sapiunt, ad terram retrahere luxoriosi conantur."

11. Augustine, *Sermo IV, De Jacob et Esau*, XI (Migne, *P.L.*, XXXVIII, 38[D]–39[B]): "Jam videte quia senuerat Isaac. Cujus personam gessit Isaac, quando voluerit benedicere filium suum majorem (Genesis 27:1)? Jam senuerat: ubi senectus, vetustas; per senectutem intelligo Vetus Testamentum. Hoc ergo Vetus Testamentum quia illi non intelligebant, qui sub nube fuerunt, ideo dicuntur caligasse oculi Isaac. Caligo oculorum corporis Isaac, caliginem significat mentium Judaeorum: senectus Isaac, vetustatem significat Veteris Testamenti. Quid ergo, fratres? Vult tamen benedicere et majorem filium Esau. Minorem amabat mater, et majorem pater, tanquam primogenitum: nam aequalis in ambos justitia, sed erat charitas major erga primogenitum. Vult ille benedicere majorem, quia Vetus Testamentum primo populo promittebat. Promissiones non loquitur nisi ad Ju-

daeos: ipsis videtur promittere, ipsis videtur omnia polliceri. Vocantur ab Aegypto, liberantur ab hostibus, per mare ducuntur, pascuntur manna, accipiunt Testamentum, accipiunt Legem, accipiunt promissiones, accipiunt ipsam terram repromissionis. Non mirum quia ille benedicere voluit primum filium: sed sub figura majoris benedicitur minor. Mater enim typum gestat Ecclesiam." ["For behold, Isaac was aged. What role did Isaac play when he wished to bless his elder son (Genesis 27:1)? For he was aged: for aged, read old; by his age, I understand the Old Testament. The Old Testament, then, since they who were in its darkness [literally, under its cloud] did not understand it, is signified by the blindness of Isaac's eyes. [Cf. John 1:5.] The blindness of Isaac's bodily eyes signifies the blindness of mind of the Jews: the aged Isaac signifies the senescence of the Old Testament. What then, brothers? He wished to bless his elder son, Esau. The mother loved the younger, and the father the elder, inasmuch as he was the firstborn: his justice was equal for both, but his love was greater for the firstborn. Just as he wished to bless the elder, so the Old Testament was a covenant with the first people. Its promises were made to none but the Jews: with them was the covenant made, to them were all its promises given. They were called out of Egypt, they were liberated from their enemies, they were led across the sea, they were fed on manna, they received the Testament, they received the Law, they received the promises, they received the promised land. No wonder he wished to bless his first son: but in the guise of the elder he blessed the younger. For the mother indeed represented and typified the church."]

Quid ergo, fratres et sorores? How new is the New Criticism?

12. Zeno, *De Somnio Jacob* (Migne, *P.L.*, XI, 428A): "Jacob habet imaginem Christi."

13. Augustine, *Sermones Supposititios*, XII, "De Beato Jacob" (Migne, *P.L.*, XXXVIII, 1762[D]): "Frequenter charitate vestrae suggessimus, fratres dilectissimi, beatum Jacob typum habuisse et figuram Domini Salvatoris."

14. Plato, *Republic*, III, 398A.

15. Bruno of Asti, *Expositio in Genesim* (Migne, *P.L.*, CLXIV, 173C): "Hoc autem signum membrorum tremor fuisse dicitur, quia quasi insaniens, et melancholico similis, ad miseriam sui homines provocabat." ["That sign was said to be a shaking of the limbs, as if he were insane, and a melancholy aspect, which aroused men's pity for him."] Cf. Isidore of Seville, *Allegoriae Quaedam Sacrae Scripturae* (Migne, *P.L.*, LXXXIII, 99C): ". . . itaque Cain vagus et profugus erat in

terra, vel στένων καὶ τρέμων—id est, gemens et tremens." ["Thus Cain was a vagabond and a fugitive in the earth, and even στένων καὶ τρέμων—that is, sighing and moaning and trembling."]

16. Ambrose, *De Cain et Abel*, I, i, 4 (Migne, *P.L.*, XIV, 317C: "Denique Rebecca . . . duas naturas humani ingenii parturiret, unam mali, alteram boni, . . . (Esau enim typus erat malitiae, Jacob figuram bonitatis gerebat)."

17. *Stephen Hero* (New York, 1955), p. 146. That Stephen's attitude toward religion was Joyce's own is indicated by J. F. Byrne, *Silent Years* (New York, 1953), pp. 85–87.

18. The saying had many forms. Cf., for example, Anselm of Canterbury, *Carmen de Contemptu Mundi* (Migne, *P.L.*, CLVIII, 689A):

Nec tonsura facit monachum, non horrida vestis;
Sed virtus animi, perpetuusque rigor.
[Neither the tonsure nor the hair shirt makes a monk;
But strength of soul, and unending rigor.]

19. See Kenneth Burke, *A Rhetoric of Motives* (New York, 1950), p. 328.

CHAPTER VI

1. See, for example, Stanislaus Joyce, *Recollections of James Joyce* (New York, 1950), pp. 6–7, 9; *My Brother's Keeper: James Joyce's Early Years* (New York, 1958), pp. 48–49; Herbert Gorman, *James Joyce* (New York, 1948), pp. 47, 297, 302; Horace Kallen, *Art and Freedom* (New York, 1942), II, 805.

2. See *The Text of the Spiritual Exercises of Saint Ignatius*, trans. by Henry Keane, S.J. (London, 1952), pp. 22–23 and *passim*. The "first prelude" to any spiritual exercise is a "composition of place. . . . In contemplation or meditation on visible matters, . . . the composition will be to see with the eyes of the imagination the corporeal place where the thing I wish to contemplate is found. . . . In meditation on invisible things . . . the composition will be to see with the eyes of the imagination and to consider that my soul is imprisoned in this corruptible body, and my whole self in this vale of misery."

3. *Letters and Instructions of St. Ignatius Loyola*, trans. by D. F. O'Leary (St. Louis and London, 1914), I, 95, 98.

4. *Constitutiones Societatis Jesu cum Declarationibus* (Antwerp, 1635),

pp. 233–234: "ut sancta Obedientia tum in executione, tum in voluntate, tum in intellectu sit in nobis semper omni ex parte perfecta;
cum magnâ celeritate, spirituali gaudio, & perseverantiâ, quidquid
nobis injunctum fuerit, obeundo; omnia justa esse, nobis persua-
dendo; omnem sententiam ac judicium nostrum contrarium caecâ
quadam Obedientiâ abnegando; & id quidem in omnibus, quae à
Superiore disponuntur, ubi definiri non possit (quemadmodum dic-
tum est) aliquod peccati genus intercedere. Et sibi quisque persua-
deat, quòd qui sub Obedientiâ vivunt, se ferri ac regi à divinâ pro-
videntiâ per Superiores suos, sinere debent, perinde ac si cadaver
essent, quod quoquoversus ferri, & quacumque ratione tractari se
sinit: vel similiter atque senis baculus, qui ubicumque, & quacūque
in re velit eo uti qui eum manu tenet, ei inservit. Si enim obediens
rem quamcumque, cui eum Superior ad auxilium totius corporis
Religionis velit impendere, cum animi hilaritate debet exequi, pro
certo habens, quòd eâ ratione potiùs, quàm re aliâ quavis, quam
praestare possit, propriam voluntatem ac judicium diversum sec-
tando, divinae voluntati respondebit."

5. *St. Ignatius and the Ratio Studiorum,* ed. by Edward A. Fitzpatrick
(New York and London, 1933), pp. 93–94.

6. *Ibid.,* pp. 164–165.

7. *Ibid.,* p. 168.

8. *Constitutiones,* pp. 118–119: "Doctrinae igitur differentes non ad-
mittantur. . . . unio vero & conformitas mutua diligentissimè cu-
randa est; nec, quae ei adversantur, permittenda."

9. *St. Ignatius and the Ratio Studiorum,* pp. 66–67.

10. *Ibid.,* p. 187.

11. See Kenneth Burke, *A Rhetoric of Motives* (New York, 1950), pp.
154–157.

12. *Text of the Spiritual Exercises,* pp. 8–9.

13. *Ibid.,* p. 14.

14. *Ibid.,* pp. 14–15.

15. *Ibid.,* p. 20.

16. *Letters and Instructions,* I, 67. Cf. I, 95, 98, on Christ's pay to His
soldiers.

17. *Text of the Spiritual Exercises,* p. 27.

18. See, for example, *The Minor Poems of the Vernon Manuscript,
Part I,* ed. by Carl Horstman (EETS No. 98); *The Minor Poems of
the Vernon Manuscript, Part II,* ed. by F. J. Furnivall (EETS No.
117); *An Old English Miscellany,* ed. by Richard Morris (EETS No.
49); *English Lyrics of the XIIIth Century,* ed. by Carleton Brown

(Oxford, 1932); *Political, Religious, and Love Poems,* ed. by F. J. Furnivall (EETS No. 15); *Selections from Early Middle English,* ed. by Joseph Hall (Oxford, 1920); *Robert of Brunne's "Handlyng Synne"* . . . , ed. by F. J. Furnivall (EETS No. 119).

19. Ch. LXIV (J.-P. Migne, *Patrologia Latina,* CLVIII, 210B): "Videtur mihi hujus tam sublimis rei secretum transcendere omnem intellectus aciem humani: et idcirco conatum explicandi qualiter hoc sit, continendum puto. Sufficere namque debere existimo rem incomprehensibilem indiganti, si ad hoc ratiocinando pervenerit ut eam certissme esse cognoscat; etiamsi penetrare nequeat intellectu, quomodo ita sit: nec idcirco minus his adhibendam fidei certitudinem, quae probationibus necessariis, nulla alia repugnante ratione asserentur; si suae naturalis altitudinis incomprehensibilitate explicari non patiantur." ["The mystery of so sublime a thing seems to me to escape all the sharpness of the human intellect: and therefore I think I shall refrain from any attempt to explain how it is. For I esteem it sufficient, for one who is investigating an incomprehensible thing, if his reasoning shall have brought him to recognize that it most certainly exists, even if his intellect is unable to understand how it exists: nor should the certitude of faith be less readily offered to those things which are asserted as necessary truths, if they are not otherwise repugnant to reason, though because of their natural sublimity they cannot be explained."]

20. *Text of the Spiritual Exercises,* p. 27.

21. *Ibid.,* pp. 130–134. Cf. George Orwell on "blackwhite," *1984* (New York: New American Library, 1953), p. 161.

22. In terms of area, Los Angeles is the largest city in the United States; in *Finnegans Wake,* the villains always think in terms of space. Beeton was one of many small communities swallowed up by Los Angeles' growth. On "poncif," see Baudelaire, *Fusées,* XIII.

23. *Text of the Spiritual Exercises,* pp. 26–27.

24. Dorothea Waley Singer, *Giordano Bruno, His Life and Thought* (New York, 1950), p. 179.

25. Kevin Sullivan informs me that the original of this phrase is "Laus Deo semper [Praise God forever]: a pious ejaculation often affixed to themes by Jesuit students."

26. See Clarence C. Green, "The Paradox of the Fall in *Paradise Lost,*" *MLN,* LIII, 8 (December, 1938), 557–571.

27. See "The Day of the Rabblement," quoted by Gorman, p. 73.

28. *Within a Budding Grove* (New York: Modern Library), Part I, p. 318.

29. *Text of the Spiritual Exercises*, p. 23.

30. Rudolph Von Abele, "*Ulysses:* The Myth of Myth," *PMLA*, LXIX, 3 (June, 1954), 364.

31. *Axel's Castle* (New York and London, 1931), pp. 200–202.

32. *James Joyce: A Critical Introduction* (Norfolk, Conn., 1941), pp. 131–132.

CHAPTER VII

1. The parenthetical references to the *Summa Theologica* are to the official translation by Fathers of the English Dominican Province (2d ed.; London, 1922–1937).

2. Reviewing a book of patriotic verse, Joyce wrote, "A man who writes a book cannot be excused by his good intentions, or by his moral character; he enters into a region where there is question of the written word." Cf. *The Early Joyce: The Book Reviews, 1902–1903*, ed. by Stanislaus Joyce and Ellsworth Mason (Colorado Springs, Colo., 1955), p. 8.

3. Virginia Woolf, *A Writer's Diary* (New York, 1954), p. 49.

4. This is exemplified by the most characteristic modern music, which is addressed primarily to the mind rather than to what the theologians used to call the concupiscence of the ear.

5. This statement also had an Arabic source. Cf. Robert Hammond, *The Philosophy of Alfarabi and Its Influence on Medieval Thought* (New York, 1947), p. 42.

6. Sylvia Beach, "Ulysses à Paris," *Mercure de France*, CCCIX (May, 1950), 16.

7. Stuart Gilbert, "Souvenirs de voyage," *Mercure de France*, CCCIX (May, 1950), 39.

8. H. A. Daniel, *Thesaurus Hymnologicus* (Leipzig, 1855), I, 251.

9. At this one point I depart from the official translation, which seems to me to put the contrast less sharply. The original reads: "bonum dicatur id quod simpliciter complacet appetitui; pulchrum autem dicatur id cuius ipsa apprehensio placet." Tolstoy, summing up the aesthetic theories of his day, makes a strikingly similar statement without any reference to Aquinas: "We recognize as beauty what pleases us, without exciting our desires." (*What Is Art?* trans. by Charles Johnston [Philadelphia, 1898], p. 60.)

10. Cf. Augustine, *The City of God,* XIX, 13, trans. by Marcus Dods (New York: Modern Library, 1950), p. 690; Aristotle, *Nicomachean Ethics,* X, 3.

11. "The Holy Office." Quoted by Herbert Gorman, *James Joyce* (New York, 1948), p. 140.

12. On the values in Western movies, cf. Robert Warshow, "The Westerner," *Partisan Review,* XXI, 2 (March–April, 1954), 190–203.

13. Gorman, p. 150.

14. William of Malmesbury, *De Gestis Pontificum Anglorum,* ed. by N. E. S. A. Hamilton (London: Rolls Series, 1870), p. 357.

15. Robert of Brunne, *Handlyng Synne,* ed. by F. J. Furnivall (London: EETS No. 119, 1901), pp. 238–240.

16. "Joyce, Nietzsche, and Hauptmann in James Joyce's 'A Painful Case,'" *PMLA,* LXVIII, 1 (March, 1953), 95–102.

17. Gorman, p. 73.

18. He follows, in fact, the instructions for directors of retreats in St. Ignatius Loyola's *Spiritual Exercises;* cf. Chapter VI.

19. See Gerhard Friedrich, "Bret Harte as a Source for James Joyce's 'The Dead,'" *Philological Quarterly,* XXXIII (1954), 442–444.

20. *Poetry and Prose of William Blake,* ed. by Geoffrey Keynes (London and New York, 1927), p. 197.

21. For *sac,* see the DuCange *Glossarium Mediae et Infimae Latinitatis;* and cf. *soca,* 4.

22. Tolstoy, *What Is Art?* pp. 161–163. Baudelaire denied any spiritual value to the sacred prostitution of the pagans, which he said was the result merely of "nervous excitation." He also said, "Sex is the lyricism of the people" (*Mon coeur mis à nu,* IV; XXXIX).

23. Cf. Rufus W. Mathewson, Jr., "The Soviet Hero and the Literary Heritage," *American Slavic and East European Review,* VII, 4 (December, 1953), 505–523. In the good society according to T. S. Eliot, things would be no better. Cf. *The Idea of a Christian Society* (London, 1939), pp. 91–92.

CHAPTER VIII

1. *De Doctrina Christiana,* II, 40; IV, 2 (J.-P. Migne, *Patrologia Latina,* XXXIV, 63[C], 63[A], 89[D]–90[A]): "in usum convertanda Christianum. . . . in usum nostrum vindicanda. . . . Cum ergo sit in

medio posita facultas eloquii, quae ad persuadenda seu prava seu recta valet plurimum; cur non bonorum studio comparatur, ut militet veritati . . . ?" ["Converting them to a Christian use. . . . claiming them for our use. . . . Since therefore the faculty of eloquence is neutral, and very strong in the service of either right or wrong convictions, why should it not be joined to the zeal for good, that it may fight for truth . . . ?"]

2. *De Oratore,* I, i, vii–viii; II, xx, 85; II, xliii, 182.

3. *Institutio Oratoria,* X, i, 1.

4. *De Doctrina Christiana,* IV, 15, 16, 27, 28 (Migne, *P.L.,* XXXIV, 103[A]–104[D], 118[A]–120[C]).

5. *Liber de Praescriptionibus Adversus Haereticos,* VII (Migne, *P.L.,* II, 20B–21A): "Quid ergo Athenis et Hierosolymis? quid Academiae et Ecclesiae? quid haereticis et Christianis? . . . Nobis curiositate opus non est, post Christum Jesum; nec inquisitione, post Evangelium." Cf. II Corinthians 6:14–16.

6. *De Doctrina Christiana,* II, 18, 40 (Migne, *P.L.,* XXXIV, 49[D], 63[A-B]): "imo verus quisquis bonus verusque christianus est, Domini sui esse intelligat, ubicumque invenerit veritatem. . . . Philosophi autem qui vocantur, si qua forte et fidei nostrae accommodata dixerunt, maxime Platonici [i.e., the Neo-Platonists], non solum formidanda non sunt, sed ab eis etiam tanquam injustis possessoribus in usum nostrum vindicanda. . . . Sic doctrinae omnes Gentilium . . . etiam liberales disciplinas usui veritatis aptiores, et quaedam morum praecepta utilissima continent, deque ipso uno Deo colendo nonnulla vera inveniuntur apud eos." ["Let everyone who is a good and true Christian know that truth is the truth of his Lord, wheresoever it be found. . . . If those who are called philosophers, especially the Platonists [i.e., the Neo-Platonists], have happened to say anything conformable to our faith, these things not only are not to be feared but are to be claimed from their unjust possessors for our use. . . . So with all branches of pagan learning. . . . they include the liberal disciplines, which are better suited to the service of truth, and contain some most useful precepts of morality; and even for the worship of the one God some true things are found among them."]

7. *De Musica,* VI, xvii, 59 (Migne, *P.L.,* XXXII, 1194[A]): "Quod tamen facere non auderemus, nisi multos pios Ecclesiae catholicae matris optimae filios, qui puerilibus studiis loquendi ac disserendi facultatem quantum satis est consecuti essent, eadem refellendorum haereticorum necessitate fecisse videremus." ["Which, however, we should not dare to do, if we had not seen that many pious sons of

that best of mothers, the Catholic Church, who in their useful studies have attained sufficient skill in speaking and disputing, have done it from the necessity of confuting heretics."]

8. *Ibid.*, VI, xi, 29 (Migne, *P.L.*, XXXII, 1179[D]): "Ita coelestibus terrena subjecta, orbes temporum suorum numerosa successione quasi carmini universitatis associant." ["Just as earthly things are subject to heavenly, so the circuits of their times and seasons join in melodious succession, as it were in a song of the universe."]

9. *Ibid.*, 1179[D]–1180[A-B]: "In quibus multa nobis videntur inordinata et perturbata, quia eorum ordini pro nostris meritis assuti sumus, nescientes quid de nobis divina providentia pulchrum gerat. Quoniam si quis, verbi gratia, in amplissimarum pulcherrimarumque aedium uno aliquo angulo tanquam statua collocetur, pulchritudinem illius fabricae sentire non poterit, cujus et ipse pars erit. Nec universi exercitus ordinem miles in acie valet intueri. Et in quolibet poemate si quanto spatio syllabae sonant, tanto viverent atque sentirent, nullo modo illa numerositas et contexti operis pulchritudo eis placeret, quam totam perspicere atque approbare non possent, cum de ipsis singulis praetereuntibus fabricata esset atque perfecta. Ita peccantem hominem ordinavit Deus turpem, non turpiter. Turpis enim factus est voluntate, universum amittendo quod Dei praeceptis obtemperans possidebat, et ordinatus in parte est, ut qui legem agere noluit, a lege agatur. . . . quia et in malis operibus nostris Dei opera bona sunt." ["In which many things seem to us disordered and perturbed, for we are fixed in their order according to our merits, not knowing what beauty divine providence will bring forth by means of us. If, for example, a statue were placed in a corner of an exceedingly large and beautiful building, it could not see the beauty of the architect's plan, for it would itself be part of it. Nor can a soldier in the front line observe the order of the whole army. And in any poem, if the syllables lived and felt while they were sounding, their melody and the beauty of their context would by no means be apparent to them; they would not be able to perceive or approve the whole, since it would be formed and perfected by the passing of each single one of them. Thus God ordains that the sinful man shall be base, but not basely. For he is made base by his own will, by giving up the integrity which he possessed when he obeyed God's precepts; he is cast in the role of one who will not fulfill the law, that the law may be fulfilled upon him. . . . For God's good works subsist even in our bad works."]

10. *Enchiridion de Fide, Spe et Charitate*, C, CI (Migne, *P.L.*, XL,

279[B], [C]): "Quantum enim ad ipsos attinet, quod Deus noluit fecerunt; quantum vero ad omnipotentiam Dei, nullo modo id efficere valuerunt. Hoc quippe ipso quod contra voluntatem facerunt ejus, de ipsis facta est voluntas ejus. . . . Nam Deus quasdam voluntates suas, utique bonas[,] implet per malorum hominum malas." ["As far as they themselves were concerned, they did what God did not wish; but as far as God's omnipotence was concerned, they could by no means succeed in doing it. By the very fact that they acted against His will, His will concerning them was fulfilled. . . . For God achieves certain of His purposes, which are of course good, through the evil wills of evil men."]

11. *Contra Epistolam Manichaei Quam Vocant Fundamenti*, XLI, 47 (Migne, *P.L.*, XLII, 205[D]): "Nam et species vocis emissae praeterit, et silentio perimitur; et tamen sermo noster ex praeteriuntium verborum decessione ac successione peragitur, et moderatis silentiorum intervallis decenter suaviterque distinguitur: ita sese habet etiam temporalium naturarum infima pulchritudo, ut rerum transitu peragatur, et distinguatur morte nascentium."

12. *De Musica*, VI, xvii, 56 (Migne, *P.L.*, XXXII, 1191[B]): "Deus autem summe bonus, et summe justus, nulli invidet pulchritudini, quae sive damnatione animae, sive regressione, sive permansione fabricatur."

13. *Enchiridion*, XCIX (Migne, *P.L.*, XL, 278).

14. *Yorkshire Writers: Richard Rolle of Hampole and His Followers*, ed. by C. Horstman[n] (London, 1896), II, xxx: "Mundi amatores scire possunt verba vel carmina nostrarum cantionum, non autem cantica nostrorum carminium." ["Lovers of the world can understand the words or verses of our song, but not the song of our verses."]

15. William James, *The Varieties of Religious Experience* (New York: Modern Library, n.d.), pp. 377–378.

16. *The Early Joyce: The Book Reviews, 1902–1903*, ed. by Stanislaus Joyce and Ellsworth Mason (Colorado Springs, Colo., 1955), p. 15.

17. For an orthodox resolution of the paradox of God's foreknowledge and man's free will, cf. *Enchiridion*, XXX, CIV, CV (Migne, *P.L.*, XL, 246[C]–247[B], 281 [B-D]).

18. *Enchiridion*, XCIX (Migne, *P.L.*, XL, 278[D]): "Si enim haec non capit, quis est qui respondet Deo? Si autem capit, magis non invenit quid respondeat. Videt enim, si capit, universum genus humanum tam justo judicio divino in apostatica radice damnatum, ut etiamsi nullus inde liberaretur, nemo recte posset Dei vituperare justitiam; et qui liberantur, sic opportuisse liberari, ut ex pluribus non liberatis,

atque in damnatione justissima derelictis, ostenderetur quid meruisset universa conspersio, et quo etiam istos debitum judicium Dei duceret, nisi eis indebita misericordia subveniret: ut volentium de suis meritis gloriari, *omne os obstruatur* [Romans 3:19]; et *qui gloriatur, in Domino glorietur"* [I Corinthians 1:31]. ["If indeed he does not understand these things, who is he to answer back to God? If he does understand them, he finds nothing more to reply. For indeed he sees, if he understands, that the whole human race was condemned in its apostate root by a judgment so just that even if none had been redeemed no one could rightly have censured God's justice; and those who are redeemed are redeemed in a way best designed to show, by the greater number who are not redeemed but left in most just damnation, what the whole race merits, and where the deserved judgment of God would lead even the redeemed, did not His undeserved mercy save them: so that 'every mouth may be stopped' [Romans 3:19] of those who would glory in their own merits; and 'He that glorieth, let him glory in the Lord' " [I Corinthians 1:31].]

Index

Abel, analogous to Esau, 65; analogous to Jacob, 65; and Cain, 46, 48, 49
Abelard, 8, 11
Abraham, 49
Adam, 39–42, 50
"After the Race," 73, 104
Aldhelm, 103
ALP, 44, 58, 81; unity with HCE, 42–43
Ambrose, Saint, 48–49, 58
Anselm of Canterbury, Saint, 7, 8, 9, 18, 47, 77
Anti-urbanism, 49
Apollo, 83
Aquinas, Saint Thomas, 9–10, 33; on active intellect, 94; on amorality of art, 91–92; on concupiscible and irascible powers of soul, 95–96; on fortitude, 97–102; on goodness and beauty, 96; on passivity of human intellect, 93; as poet, 90–91; on subject matter of art, 93
"Araby," 104
Aristotle, 6, 33, 38, 45, 53, 56, 90, 98, 134; on arts and virtues, 91, 92; on subject matter of art, 93
Arius, 26
Arnold, Matthew, 117
Artist, alienation, 238; analogous to God, 21–22, 45–46, 135, 136, 138
Augustine, Saint, 6, 9, 45, 49, 58–59, 60, 80, 81; on categories of sin, 24; and free will, Chap. VIII *passim;* on God as artist, 21–22, Chap. VIII *passim;* on predestination, 27; on rhetoric, Chap. VIII *passim*
Averroes, 71, 113
Ayenbite of Inwyt, Chap. II *passim*

Bacon, Roger, 9
Barabbas, 137
Baudelaire, 22, 46
Benedict, Saint, 103
Berengar of Tours, 5, 6, 7, 14
Black Liz, 39
Blake, William, 114
Blind piano tuner, 30
Bloom, Leopold, defiance, 83–85, 86; detachment, 31; fortitude, 113, 118; future, 86; as gentleman, 85; as God the Father, 19, 35; intellectual curiosity, 32–33; as Jew, 27, 33, 84; kindness, 118; need for acceptance, 24, 27, 83–85; relations with Stephen, 88; sins, 18, 23, 28–29, 31–32; substitution, 24; superiority, 27; as Tempter, 20; as thinker, 32–33, 117
Bloom, Molly, future course, 85–86; seedcake, 19, 38
"Boarding House, The," 105–6
Boylan, 83, 85, 86, 137
Breen, Mrs. Denis, 38

Brothers Karamazov, The, 86, 100

Bruno, Giordano, 80

Burrus, as Shaun, 123; and Caseous, 48, 82

Burton restaurant, 29

Byrne, Davy, 29

Byron, George Gordon, 46

Caesar, Julius, 128

Cain, 103; analogous to Esau, 65; analogous to Jacob, 64–65; *see also* Abel

Camus, Albert, 87

Cannibal chief, 38

Carrouges, Michel, 19

Caseous, alienation, 122; as Shem, 122–23; *see also* Burrus

Cato, 128

Chandler, Tommy, 73–74, 105

Chapelain, Jean, 54

Chuff, 63; and Glugg, 52, 54, 82; as Shaun and Shem, 57

Church, as enemy of spiritual life, 4–5, 23, 45, 65, 70, 82

Cicero, 98, 128

Citizen, The, 27

Claudel, Paul, 45

"Clay," 110

Clifford, Martha, 31

Cohen, Bella, 39, 85

Confucius, 53

Conmee, Father John, 24, 60

Conroy, Gabriel, 109, 110

Corley, Lord John, 104–5, 115

Costello, Punch, 24

"Counterparts," 107

Cowley, Father Bob, 30

Cranly, 4, 12, 133

Cunningham, Martin, 109

Cyprian, Saint, 54

Davin, 112

"Day of the Rabblement, The," 120

"Dead, The," 109–10

Deasy, Garret, 45

Dedalus, Dilly, 34

Dedalus, Simon, 19

Dedalus, Mrs. Simon, 34, 116

Dedalus, Stephen, alienation, 20, 138; on artist's role, 124; confession, 76–77; cunning, 112; debt to Aquinas, 91; debt to Augustine, 127, 132; defiance, 86; desire to join Jesuits, 70; emotionalism, 94–95; fortitude, 110–17; as god, 34; as God the Son, 19, 20–21; as godlike artist, 33; identifies himself with Jews, 46; with Trinity, 34; independence of mind, 4; on Irish Catholicism, 65, 70; and Jesuits, 20; on language, 133–34; need for freedom, 24, 37, 117; non-artistic aim, 100, 112, 138; obedience in school, 72; and Orestes, 21; rebellion against Jesuit ideal, 73; recognition of claims of world, 86; religious doubts, 4; religious sensibility, 4, 22–23, 121; seeming orthodoxy, 26, 27; sins, 17, 34–35, 76–77

Didacticism, 99–100

Dignam, Patrick, 34

Dignam, Mrs. Patrick, 24

Dillon, Leo, 104

Dolan, Father, 131

Dollard, Ben, 30

Dolph, 63; as Antichrist, 82; and Kev, 81–82

Doran, Bob, 105-6

Douce, Miss Lydia, 30
Doyle, Jimmy, 73, 104
Duffy, James, 107
Duns Scotus, John, 3, 9, 10, 11

Eliot, T. S., 22, 77, 92, 126
"Encounter, An," 104
Enoch, 49
Entelechy, 34, 36
Epiphanies, 36
Erigena, John Scotus, 5, 9, 21,
    Chap. III *passim;* on the sexes,
    39
Eucharist, 4, 6, 7, 13–15; in cab-
    men's shelter, 20; at hands of
    prostitute, 116
Eve, 40–42
Eveline, 73
"Eveline," 104
Exiles, 41

Farrington, 73, 107
Faust, 61
Flaubert, on godlike artist, 21
Florry, 116
Flynn, the Rev. James, 103
Flynn, Nosey, 29
Francis of Assisi, Saint, 13
Frazer, Sir James G., 19
Fromm, Erich, 49
Furey, Michael, 109–10

Gallaher, Ignatius, 74, 106–7, 115
"Gas from a Burner," 38
Gea-Tellus, 86
Gessner, Salomon, 46
Glugg, 60; *see also* Chuff
Gonzaga, Vespasiano, 78–79
Goulding, Richie, 31
"Grace," 59, 62, 108–9

Gracehoper, and Ondt, 48, 52–53,
    81, 82; as Shem and Shaun, 57
Grand Inquisitor, 48, 68, 86
Gregory, Lady, 115
Gripes, and Mookse, 39, 48, 51,
    79, 80–81; as Shem and Shaun,
    57

Hades, 53
Haines, 26, 27, 115
Hamlet, 34, 87
Handlyng Synne, 17
Hathaway, Anne, 39
HCE, 42, 56, 58, 80, 81; *see also*
    ALP
Heraclitus, 56, 127
Hoffer, Eric, 69
Humanitas, 5, 7, 10, 12
Huxley, Aldous, 77–78, 79

Icarus, 19
In His Steps, 100
Isaac, 56, 57, 58, 59, 66
Isidore, Bishop of Seville, 49
"Ivy Day in the Committee
    Room," 107–8

Jacob, 64, 112
James, William, 132
Jerome, Saint, 9
Jerry, and Kevin, 64
Jesuits, abnegation of private
    judgment, 78; accommodation
    to facts, 73–76; anti-individual-
    ism, 77–79, 80; appeal to busi-
    nessmen, 109; obedience, 69–71
Joan of Arc, 54
John XXII, Pope, 12–13
John of Salisbury, 8, 11, 53
Joyce, James, aesthetics, falsity of,
    124–26; alienation, 121–23; anti-

Joyce, James (*continued*)
theist, 19; on art, 18–19; on artist's role, 97; attitude toward church, 5; debt to Aquinas, 90–95; debt to Augustine, 127; emotionalism, 95; fortitude, 121; impiety, 46; on morality, 18–19; on nature of artist, 21; on pornographic and didactic art, 97; renunciation of his education, 70; romanticism, 125, 136; on sex, 41; on unity of history, 34–36, 39; on unity of sexes, 42; use of Aquinas on fortitude, 103–10

Justius, and Mercius, 46, 47, 51, 82; as Shaun and Shem, 57

Jute, and Mutt, 56; as Esau and Jacob, 62

Kearney, Mr., 108
Kearney, Mrs., 73, 108
Kearney, Kathleen, 73, 108
Kernan, Tom, 108–9
Kevin, 63, 80; *see also* Jerry

Lanfranc, 7
La Pucelle, 54
La Pucelle d'Orléans, 54
Leapyear Girls, 51, 52, 60–63, 81, 137
Lenehan, 24, 56, 88, 105, 115
Levin, Harry, 86
Lollards, 15
Lot, 49
Loyola, Saint Ignatius of, 16, Chap. VI *passim; see also* Jesuits
Luther, Martin, 13
Lynch, 90, 125

McCann, 133
MacDowell, Gerty, 85
MacHale, Cardinal, 62
Macrobius, 98
MacTrigger, the Rev. Mr., 38
Magalaner, Marvin, 107
Magdalen, Mary, 116
Maimonides, 113
Mann, Charles, 49
Man's alienation from nature, 18, 50
Margareta, 61
Maria, 110
Marx, Karl, 80, 84
Mendelssohn, Felix, 84
Menton, John Henry, 83
Mercius, *see* Justius
Michael da Cesena, 12
Michel, Dan, 30
Milkwoman, 26
Mookse, 60; identifies himself with God, 79; *see also* Gripes
Mooney, Mrs., 105
Mooney, Jack, 106
Mooney, Polly, 105
Moral neutrality of universe, 18
Moses, 47
Most, Johann, 27
"Mother, A," 108
Moynihan, 131, 137
Mulligan, Malachi, 20–21, 23, 24, 25–27, 68, 89, 115, 137
Mutt, 66; *see also* Jute

Nebuchadnezzar, 123
Nero, 123
Newman, John Henry Cardinal, 92, 93

Obedience, in *Dubliners*, 73–74
Oedipus, 87

Ondt, 63; *see also* Gracehoper
O'Neill, Hugh and Owen Roe, 54
Ormond bar, 31, 137
Ortega y Gasset, José, 77, 78
Orwell, George, 100

"Painful Case, A," 107
Parnell, Charles Stewart, 108
Pater, Walter, 92
Persephone, 53
Photius, 23, 26, 27
Piers Plowman, 17
Plato, 39, 86, 126
Pound, Ezra, 126
Proto-Protestantism, 3, 5, 10–11,
    13, 15
Proust, Marcel, 83
Purdon, Father, 59, 74, 75, 109

Quintilian, 128, 129

Rainbow Girls, 54, 60
Ratio Studiorum, 70–71
Realist-Nominalist controversy,
    Chap. I *passim*
Rebecca, 58, 59; analogous to Eve,
    65
Richards, Grant, 100
Rolle, Richard, 8, 131
Roscellinus of Compiègne, 7
Rupert, Abbot of Tuitium, 49

Sabellius, 26
Saint Albans, chronicler of, 15
Salinger, J. D., 99
Sancho Panza, 80
Shakespeare, 27, 38–39
Shaun, as Abel and Cain, 50 ff.; as
    Esau and Jacob, 65; identifies

himself with Mookse, 79; and
    Shem, 20, 43, 46, 48, 87, 88, 137;
    interdependence, 66
Shem, alienation, 123; his book,
    65–66; taste in food, 64; lack of
    dogmatism, 87; *see also* Shaun
Siegfried, 116
"Sisters, The," 103
Socrates, 79, 80
Solon, 122
Spinoza, 84
Spiritual Exercises, 74–79
Swift, Jonathan, 39

Tertullian, 4, 32, 128
Throwaway, 120
Trinity, 7, 8, 34
Triv and Quad, 80, 81
True Believer, The, 69

Unity of history, 34–36
Unity of opposites, 39, 64–67, **88**
Unity of sexes, 42
Unmoved Mover, 19, 45

Valentine, 26
Valéry, Paul, 87
Voltaire, 54

Waugh, Evelyn, 77
Wilde, Oscar, 92, 125
William of Ockham, 11–14, 77
Wilson, Edmund, 86
Woolf, Virginia, 92
Wyclif, John, 3, 11–15

Xenophon, 51

Zeno, Bishop of Verona, 60